£1

The

CN00904747

biography.

Outback
Women

£5

Published by Brolga Publishing Pty Ltd
ABN 46 063 962 443
PO Box 12544, A'Beckett St, Victoria, Australia, 8006
email: markzocchi@brolgapublishing.com.au

National Library of Australia Cataloguing-in-Publication entry

        Author: Bugeja, Paul.
        Title: Outback women : tales of outstanding 'amazons'
        of the Australian outback / Paul Bugeja.
        ISBN: 9781925367744 (pbk.)
        Subjects: Frontier and pioneer life--Australia.
                Rural women--Australia.
                Ranchers' spouses--Australia.
                Country life--Australia.
                Australia--Rural conditions.
        Dewey Number: 305.48

Printed in Australia
Cover by David Khan
Typeset by Jade Raykovski

Outback Women

Tales of Outstanding 'Amazons' of the Australian Outback

By Paul Bugeja

DEDICATION

For the Amazons of my life.

My mother, who has supported me in all my endeavours.

My Nana Josie, who at 92 will live on, I'm sure, to be a 'centenarian amazon'

My Auntie Jacque, with whom I shared so many laughs as a child and still do.

The many female friends: you know who you are, you fearless Amazons one and all.

And, of course, for all those Amazonian women, in the city or the sticks, whose lives remain the constant challenge of balancing their roles as mother, partner, worker, citizen.

…and last, but not least, a final thank you to a small bunch of 'barista amazons' at Whileaway Café in Port Douglas, without whose excellent café lattes this book would never have been finished.

TABLE OF CONTENTS

FOREWORD

You have to accept whatever comes, and the only important thing is that you meet it with courage, and with the best that you have to give.

Eleanor Roosevelt

Taking up the challenge to put together a collection of stories about women who have had an impact, in one way or another, on the Australian outback, I discovered almost immediately an array of wonderful and amazing characters with memorable and sometimes even legendary stories.

Since its discovery, Australia has grown from penal colony to modern nation and important player on the global stage, and during this period there have been any number of women who have courageously taken on the multifarious and sometimes death-defying challenges the Aussie outback has thrown at them, often alongside the man they loved with a gaggle of children in tow.

These women have faced their trials admirably, with rarely a word of complaint, and continue to do so to this day—they are our 'Aussie Amazons'.

Given the sheer number of women who might be included in this collection, it was never my intention to cover every notable woman connected in some way to the Australian outback, and admittedly I have included reference to only one woman of something akin to an indigenous background...one could conceivably argue that every indigenous female is an Australian Amazon of sorts!

In compiling the book I have predominantly skewed it towards offering insight into a cross-section of women who took on the Aussie outback, despite it being most often alien to them, and in doing so either had some impact on the wider narrative of Australian history or produced individual, inspiring stories that should be lauded by us all.

Some of these stories I have attempted to relate in full; others are more selective in describing the more prominent moments of the individual's life. Either way, as you read, you will be astounded, intrigued and occasionally shocked by the stories.

And yet whatever your feelings I have little doubt you will share with me the sense of pride at the great achievements and Amazonian qualities of these wonderful women.

Paul Bugeja
June 2012

INTRODUCTION

Amazon / 'æm z n/ *n.*

1. A member of a mythical race of female warriors...
2. (**amazon**) a very tall, strong, or athletic woman

Oxford Concise Dictionary

True to this definition, the word 'amazon' generally conjures up images of wild and powerful warrior women, fighting off foes in some primitive matriarchal society where they rule over men who have been subverted to more menial roles.

More generally, however, it talks of simple but important character traits.

Strength.

Fortitude.

Courage.

And, maybe most importantly, grace under pressure.

All undeniable qualities of our 'Australian Amazons'.

When Captain James Cook first landed in *Terra Australis* aboard *The Endeavour* in 1770, he could have had little idea, at least initially, that he was about to lay claim to the world's largest island and smallest continent—a landmass of over 7.6 million square kilometres.

Over the decades to follow, this 'island' would be explored and navigated, with a picture of its true geographical nature slowly drawn by those who dared traverse its great expanse. In just about every corner of this 'Great Southern Land' there existed an indigenous population located in of over 40,000 years inhabitancy; there was a wide range of flora and fauna never see before or imagined; and from initial forays into the interior, the continent appeared most liveable along its coastlines, for, as explorers very quickly discovered, the vast inner heart of this massive continent was primarily desert, rocky mountainous ranges and scorched scrubland, with temperatures that soared higher than anything many of those who traversed its arid internal regions had experienced. Water was scarce, there were but two seasons—wet and dry—and the indigenous peoples were protective of their lands.

These discoveries no doubt prompted the obvious question: was this 'outback' actually uninhabitable?

Yet even with such doubts in mind, it is in man's very nature to take up the challenges an alien environment of the sort posed, and rather than be outdone to instead tame, claim and bend it to his will.

And so he did.

Edward John Eyre would be the first man, together with his indigenous guide, Wylie, to cross Southern Australia from east to west, travelling across the Nullarbor Plain from Adelaide to Albany in 1840.

Burke and Wills would similarly set out to traverse from one side of the continent to the other, although in their case from bottom to top, as they travelled from the south to the north. Sadly, their journey would infamously end under tragic circumstances, with the pair dying of starvation at Cooper Creek in 1861.

There were also the great early pastoralists—men who saw untapped potential in this new land, even in its most arid locations, where they might crow crops or raise livestock.

James Ainslie was one of the first.

In the 1820's this Scotsman, taking up some land in Duntroon in the Northern Territory, turned a herd of 700 sheep into a massive 20,000 head, before returning to Scotland in 1835.

William Buchanan came not long after.

Arriving in Australia with his family in 1837, after leasing a run with his father in New England, and following some failed attempts at gold prospecting, he began to build a pastoral empire in both NSW and the Territory, going on to become one of Australia's most renowned pioneer pastoralists.

Most famous of all, however, was John MacArthur, ex-naval officer.

By 1801 Macarthur was the largest sheep owner in the colony and would go on to help establish our wool and sheep industry with his imported merino stock, leaving a lasting legacy.

So, you might ask, while these men were exploring the outback, creating both the backbone of our agricultural industry while at the same time helping to more generally establish the nation, where were the women and what were they doing?

Simple.

They were working alongside these pioneering men, travelling with them to the far reaches of the continent; helping manage the stations and farms; running households and performing the multitude of 'duties' that had been expected of them for millennia; supporting families who needed every ounce of energy they could offer under harsh conditions; and dealing with, yet also connecting to, the indigenous peoples and, in their more intuitive feminine ways, forging positive relationships with them.

They were right there, fulfilling an extensive range of role and tasks while keeping the home fires burning, building the nation right along with their men.

And still are.

Some of the earliest female pioneers included Georgiana McRae and Emma Withnell.

The former was a promising artist from a privileged, if slightly scandal-tainted, life in London, the 'bastard' daughter of a Duke. McCrae would uproot herself for love, travel half a world away, raise a large brood of children and help husband Andrew to establish a sheep run in Arthur's seat on what later became known as the Mornington Peninsular just out of Melbourne. The same woman would be versatile enough to mix with the local Melbourne 'aristocracy' when called upon, and yet act as something of a medicine woman and friend to the local tribes of indigenous Australians residing in the region.

Emma Withnell, who would be dubbed 'the mother of the northwest', was born to a pastoralist and his wife in the far reaches of the newly forming state of Western Australia. She and husband John would travel to the north of the state in search of new opportunities, facing innumerable challenges, and yet always, like true pioneers, seeing them through and surviving the worst to go on and face whatever next might be thrown at them.

Later, there were women like Daisy Bates and Mayse Young.

Bates, a feisty liberated woman of her time, came to Australia to start a new life, and promptly did so, although initially it was unsettled and not necessarily the life of her choosing. However, in time she would commence an anthropological study of Indigenous Australians that would traverse several decades and, while being labelled as somewhat controversial in part, would end up being considered an instrumental service to the indigenous community in terms of bringing some aspects of their plight to the attention of government.

Mayse Young, on the other hand, would become renowned for quite a different 'service' to Australian society more generally—pulling beers from behind the bar! This popular outback publican owned numerous pubs in the Northern Territory at a time women business owners, particularly in the hotel industry, were a rarity, and would became renowned for her good nature and solid business head.

Moving into a more contemporary landscape, women continue to play important roles in the outback and have wonderful tales to tell.

There are the adventurers, like Robyn Davidson, famous for undertaking a solo trek through the centre of Australia, from Alice Springs to the far west coast of Australia, with just her dog and four camels for company.

The pastoralists, such as Sara Henderson, who, with ex-American-naval hero husband Charlie, would establish the massive 'Bullo Station' in the Top End of Australia and go on to become something of a local celebrity after documenting a colourful and sometimes extraordinary life in her autobiography,

From Strength to Strength.

And there are those who survive against all the odds: who look fate in the eye and dare it to stop them.

Women like Gayle Shann who, after a horrific farming accident that ripped her arm from its socket and nearly killed her, refused to lie down and accept that her life had changed forever.

Rather, she embraced this challenge and carried on regardless.

The Australian outback is filled with the stories of such extraordinary women, and there can be little doubt that many more tales will emerge in times to come as such resilient and brave women continue to do remarkable things in so many different ways under all manner of circumstance.

Colonial Amazons

(18th-19th century)

It is not easy to be a pioneer – but oh, it is fascinating! I would not trade one moment, even the worst moment, for all the riches in the world.

Elizabeth Blackwell, Scientist

New places, new countries, new worlds.

Every generation has its trail-blazers—men who know there is more than what lies immediately before them and who are compelled to go in search of it.

In many instances, there are, of course, women right alongside them.

Some of their names will be familiar, others not, but all in all they have in their own way added something great to the building of a nation we are proud of and which occupies its own special place on the world stage.

Georgiana Huntly McCrae

1804-1890

On 15 March 1804, George, Marquis of Huntly (later Duke of Gordon) and Jane Graham welcomed a daughter to the world.

And yet maybe 'welcomed' is too kind a term, as the newly-arrived infant was, in fact, illegitimate: following her birth, she was spirited away by her mother to avoid any form of scandal.

Despite this somewhat inauspicious beginning to her life, their daughter would go on to become a painter of some talent and be seen as a highly-respected woman of the new colony.

A FTER SEVERAL YEARS SPENT in quasi-exile in Scotland, in 1809 five-year-old Georgiana Huntly and her mother moved to London, establishing residence in Somers Town.

Here the small girl began her education at a convent in an area where many who had fled the French Revolution thirty years before still resided. Fears of these 'refugees' having a 'Catholic influence' on her meant Georgiana was soon moved to Claybrook House in Fulham, and later the New Road Boarding School.

Time spent in Somers Town, and the schooling she obtained while there, had its benefits. She was able to speak fluent French at an almost native level and her linguistic skills similarly lent themselves to both Latin and Hebrew. Georgiana also began to exhibit some talent as a musician, but soon discovered a different creative love to throw her energies into in the form of visual arts.

This artistic merit would be recognised and encouraged when the young girl went on to study at the Royal Academy from 1820-21 where she worked hard to develop her artistic skills, focussing on sketching and painting, and doing well enough to be awarded several medals for her work.

Finishing her studies, and faced with an ailing mother who sadly eventually passed away, much to her surprise the 16-year-old Georgiana was welcomed back into her father's house: finally, it seemed, acknowledged as a Duke's daughter.

This proved no token gesture.

Georgiana was completely reintegrated into the Duke's family and life, and years later in 1836 as his death approached he made her one of his rightful heirs, promising a sizeable portion of his estate.

Unfortunately for Georgiana, despite the Duke's good intentions in wanting to truly mark her as his kin, his will remained un-signed, and following his death, the Duchess refused to acknowledge his wishes regarding Georgiana, instead 'kindly' offering a small stipend.

The Duchess did, however, promise a large bequest to her 'step-daughter' once the Duchess herself died. One might have thought that after the 'mishap' with her father's estate Georgiana would have tried to secure this promise in writing. It remained, however, a promise in word alone, never documented, something Georgiana would rue many years later when the Duchess did eventually die.

During the time spent in her father's household, Georgiana grew into womanhood and men started showing romantic interest in her. Several different suitors came courting, the most favourable in her eyes being Peter Charles Gordon, the heir of the Laird of Wardhouse.

By the late 1820's, a marriage looked favourable, but such was not meant to be.

Their relationship was suddenly terminated, with no records, either public or private, to indicate why.

In 1829, Georgiana moved to Edinburgh where she took up painting for her first patron, Charles Kilpatrick Sharp, and within a year had made a reasonable income of £250, but remained distracted by still strong feelings for Gordon. In time she accepted that their relationship was not meant to be, and when another of her suitors, Andrew McCrae, proposed in January 1830, she accepted.

They were wed in September of that year, eventually moving to London where Andrew practiced law at Westminster. During this time, their financial situation remained somewhat precarious, and with the coming of children, Andrew's eyes turned outwards in search of a more lucrative life.

He decided his fortunes lay in the new colony, so in November 1838 he boarded *the Royal Saxon*, bound for Sydney.

Alone.

Why did he not take his wife and family?

After the recent birth of their fourth child, Georgiana remained unwell. So unwell, in fact, that such an arduous voyage could prove detrimental to both her and the newborn child.

In light of this, she and the children remained behind, with Georgiana once more painting portraits to eke out some kind of income to support her family while Andrew tried to establish himself.

Half a world away, contemplating New Zealand as a potential home, Andrew instead opted to leave Sydney for Port Philip where he began practicing law. Hearing of this in the *Port Philip Herald*, Georgiana at once began making plans to reunite the family.

This proved something of an issue, given their poor financial state, so in desperation she approached the Duchess with the aim of gaining some assistance.

To her great surprise, her pleas for help were successful.

Whether this was due to the Duchess feeling some degree of guilt about the way Georgiana had been treated after the death of the Duke, or if it was a more cynical opportunity to remove the bothersome step-daughter to somewhere so far away that it would be nigh impossible to lay claim to the estate after the Duchess' death, will never be known, although it is likely as much the latter as the former.

Regardless, money was forthcoming to pay for the entire family's one-way travel to Australia.

Setting sail with her four sons on *the Argyle* in October 1840, a four-month journey lay before them, made slightly more comfortable by the Duchess' support.

They made land in Williamston in March 1841.

Georgiana kept extensive diaries at the time, detailing as one might expect the more minute personal aspects of her life, but also, importantly, about life more generally, providing a fascinating snapshot of the state of affairs at that time in the colonies. Life in this new world was a struggle for Georgiana, especially after the large span of years she had spent in the lap of luxury at her father's wealthy estate.

Setting up home in Argyle Cottage, in Little Lonsdale St West, she found herself removed from any notion of privilege and the most basic of amenities. The cottage had an outdoor toilet; there was no real semblance of a floor, with instead mud lying under foot; and a hole in the roof was all there was to allow cooking smoke to escape the room.

A relief from this hardship was the friendship she formed with Lieutenant-Governor Charles La Trobe and his wife Sophie, with the former, it is believed, encouraging Georgiana's interest in native flora and fauna. This well-connected couple also gave the newly-arrived woman a sense of a more civilised life once more, connecting her into the small upper echelon of the social circle of new Melbourne, and their friendship would continue with her for decades.

Life improved somewhat following the birth of her first

daughter in December 1841.

A new house, Mayfield, being built for the growing family on the Yarra River (near what is now known as Studley Park), and designed by Georgiana herself, was drawing close to completion. In 1842, they moved into this much more civilised habitation, but unfortunately for Georgiana this newfound comfort would be short-lived.

Times had grown tough in Port Philip, and with still no real grasp of how to make an income large enough to support his growing family, Andrew decided to try his luck further afield. In 1843 he decided to take up the lease on the 'Arthur's Seat Run', an eight-hour journey by boat away from Port Philip.

Purchase regulations set up at the time by Governor Gipps initially obstructed McCrae's plans, but in due course he was able to negotiate a seven-year lease for an expansive run in the area. He commenced construction of a cottage at the foot of the Seat so that his family could join him, which they did in 1845 as Georgiana sat five months pregnant with her sixth child (she would go on to have two more while at Arthur's Seat, the last at the advanced age of forty-seven.)

Having to start all over yet again, Georgiana did her best to make life comfortable for her family. Being so far away from Melbourne meant she had to rely on monthly supply shipments for the household essentials, and outside of these did her best to make their life as self-sufficient as possible.

Over the next five years Georgiana embraced and settled as much as possible into her rural existence, allowing herself the occasional moment to paint after a long absence from any significant creative pursuit. Arthur's Seat also became a honeypot for artistic and literary visitors, whom she would receive as guests whenever possible.

Georgiana's hospitality was not restricted to just these occasional visitors. Over time she began forging links to the local indigenous peoples of the region, the Bunurong people. This amicable connection became so well-known in the region that other run-holders in the vicinity acknowledged her particular sensitivity with dealing with and 'managing' the locals. She took the time to learn as much of their language as possible, painted them when given permission, and even gained something of a reputation amongst them as a medicine woman.

All in all, life was fairly settled and, while still feeling somewhat the effects of isolation, Georgiana was reasonably happy with her lot...that is, until a family tragedy shook this general contentment: her daughter, Agnes, died at the age of three.

Georgiana's grieving at the loss of her beloved child hung over her for some time, and even when it lifted its dreadful pall, and she was more fully recovered, she would miss her for the rest of her days.

On rare occasions she would 'get away' to Melbourne for some short respite amongst 'society', and on one of these visits inadvertently found herself mired in a minor scandal that would throw into question her relationship with La Trobe.

Away from the Seat for two weeks, Georgiana found herself attending a series of functions on Governor La Trobe's arm as his 'official partner' when Sophie Latrobe fell ill. Although on the surface this was completely innocent, the gossip-starved colony jumped on it and whispers passed around that the pair were having an affair.

There was no substantial evidence that this was the case, and eventually the rumours subsided.

Some credence, however, might be given to this gossip. It is alleged that certain personal documents and letters of Georgiana's might support the claims of an extra-marital affair with Latrobe—letters that were destroyed, possibly at the hands of her sister, to protect Georgiana's reputation.

Returning to Arthur's Seat, life uneventfully carried on, but as though under some curse that would not allow her to stay settled for too long a period, Georgiana's life was to be upturned yet again.

The run at the Seat, no matter how hard they worked it, had not turned into the livestock goldmine Andrew hoped it would. This, combined with the frenzied advent of a gold rush in Central Victoria, which provided potential work opportunities for a financially-desperate Andrew, would eventually permanently draw Georgiana and the family back north to Melbourne, even as Andrew went off to the fields in search of work.

As Georgiana and the children settled back into 'city' life, Andrew took up duties as a police magistrate at Alberton in Gippsland, then at Barrow's Inn, Hepburn and Creswick. He finally settled in Kilmore, where he remained for the next seventeen years, also serving as warden of the goldfields and deputy-sheriff.

He retired in 1866, 'permanently' hanging up his sheriff's badge upon his death nearly a decade later in 1874.

Georgiana herself never accompanied him on his roving occupational travels and the state of their relationship during this time remains somewhat unclear as to whether the separation was due to his work or for more personal reasons, although some evidence points towards the fact that they were estranged, the separation being a mutually-agreed situation.

In her twilight years, there still lay one final chapter of misfortune to be played out in terms of Georgiana's bastardry and claims over her father's estate.

Upon the Duchess' eventual death, rather than leave Georgiana the money verbally promised so many years before, she was left not a penny. Furious, her son George returned to England to pursue a claim over the Duchess' estate, but soon realised the legal battle would be too costly, returning to Australia having secured merely a small stipend.

Despite this disappointing outcome, Georgiana remained in Melbourne for the rest of her days, living in reasonable comfort with her children until her death in 1890.

In an obituary written by scholar, teacher and journalist, Alexander Sutherland, Georgiana was offered high praise.

'It was largely due to the influence of such women as Mrs McRae that ideas of refinement and principals of taste were kept alive during the "dark ages" of our colonial history'.

Strong words from which it can be surmised that despite the harsh realities and change of lifestyle she faced when she took up with Andrew all those years before, Georgiana McRae remained as much as possible the educated, refined, daughter of Duke until her dying breath.

Isabella Mary Kelly

c. 1802 - 1872

At a time when women were mostly beholden to their husbands, and to remain unbetrothed was deemed something of an unfortunate curse, one woman cared naught for such, instead becoming a successful self-made pastoralist and well-known local figure within the region in which she lived.

In fact, so determined was she to maintain herself without the aid of a husband that she would later become renowned as the only 'single' (non-married) woman in Australia's history to be a settler in her own right.

And this she did, despite a multitude of challenges thrown at her, unsurprisingly, mostly by her male peers.

Challenges she withstood and fought against until near her dying breath.

BECOMING AN ORPHAN IS a tragedy in its own right, but such occurring at the turn of a new century in the wake of the 1798 Irish Rebellion, and the violence and unrest that came with it, must have been terrifying.

This is the unfortunate situation Isabella Mary Kelly found herself in as a child of eight.

Born in Dublin sometime between 1802 and 1806, little is known of her early life barring the sad fact of the loss of her parents while she was still a child. Following the death of her mother and father, her brother sought to right the situation, spiriting her away to London where he had arranged for her to be fostered by Sir William Crowder, a Justice of the High Court.

The kindness of he and his wife Ann allowed Isabella to be part of their family of six.

There remains scant information about her life as a young woman growing into adulthood, but it is known that when approaching her thirties Isabella sought out different climes, heading to the Colonies in 1834, with immigration records citing 'health-reasons' as the main motivation.

Before leaving for New South Wales, Isabella had spent time in Paris where she met a lady who said her daughter was married to John Plunkett, the Attorney-General of New South Wales. Having formed a brief friendship with the woman, Isabella agreed to take a parcel and a letter out to her, and these were duly delivered to Mrs Plunkett on her arrival. (This is worthy of note because much later Plunkett would prosecute a number of court cases on Isabella's behalf.)

On 29 June, along with 109 passengers, Isabella sailed upon the barque *James*, arriving in Sydney Harbour just shy of five months later. She carried with her letters of introduction to men like Macarthur, Arthur a'Beckett and his brother Sir William a'Beckett, indicating her elite connections within the colony and the potential for her to work herself into the right social circles once there.

Isabella brought with her goods and cash to the value of £2000, most of which she proceeded to sell upon her arrival as a means of acquiring more money to establish herself. Already possessing an entrepreneurial bent, she leant out some of her money as mortgages, and sometimes, when liquidity problems arose, borrowed money herself. She purchased land, including a number of speculative blocks at Maitland.

She was clearly a woman of capital and substance, and one might assume her guardian had some hand in this.

In 1839, Isabella took up residence on her 'Mount George' property. The Australian Agricultural Company (commonly known as the A. A. Company) had gained a grant of a million acres of land, extending from Port Stephens to the south bank of the Manning River. At that time, 'Mount George' was on the main route north from Maitland or Port Stephens to Gloucester and through to Port Macquarie, with numerous travellers passing up the western boundary of the A. A. Company land and crossing the Manning River at 'Mount George'.

Isabella reported she initially bought 200 head of cattle – 100 cows and 100 calves – at an auction in Maitland, and then hired four men to drive them up to 'Mount George'. With horses in short supply at the time, she paid £100 for each and £110 for one particular mare – enormous amounts in this period. She also acquired sheep.

Establishing herself in an area that would over the next twenty years or so slowly become more and more populated, as a solo woman with no apparent desire to attach herself to a male Kelly became the subject of much rumour and innuendo.

The primary gossip that circulated the district about Isabella was speculation as to her reasons for coming to the colony, with the most popular version of this venturing she was born in Dublin, with her father, a wealthy doctor there, sending her to France to finish her education.

The story went on to claim that Isabella met and fell in love with a British Army officer and they decided to get married. All the wedding arrangements had been made and it seemed everything was going to plan, but on the day of the wedding in London she turned up on time at the church only to find the groom was late.

She waited and waited, but he never arrived, so home she went, unmarried and humiliated.

According to this account, Isabella checked up on her reluctant groom – one source named him as a 'Major Wilford' – and discovered he had sailed to Sydney on Army service. She followed him there, but upon her arrival found he had swapped duty with another officer and left for India. Bereft, and in a foreign world that could be cruel to a single women, supposedly this experience made Isabella determined never to marry and to make something of herself in a male-dominated world.

Scuttling such rumours, however, was the account of her by John Allan, one of her few friendly neighbours, who made no mention of this story in writing his recollections of Kelly and spoke highly of her in general.

This is not to say Isabella's life was entirely man or love-free.

About eighteen months after her arrival at 'Mount George', someone did propose marriage to Isabella—a man by the name of Henry Flett.

In 1841, Flett, aged thirty-one, married Mary Wynter, the twenty-year-old daughter of William Wynter of Tarree, but sometime before his marriage to Wynter proposed to Kelly, who was probably about five years his senior. Isabella refused him and Flett allegedly told her that if she ever revealed his offer of marriage to anyone, he would become her most bitter enemy.

In the space of just over ten years, Flett went on to become the richest and most powerful man in the Manning Valley and a Magistrate and Member of Parliament, and true to his word, the former suitor of Isabella Mary Kelly would become one of her most bitter enemies, using his position and influence to oppose and thwart her.

This despite her never revealing the spurned proposal.

Notwithstanding such, life went on for Isabella as she managed a successful run in the Valley, but trouble arose towards the end of 1846 when she travelled to Stroud to take out a warrant for the arrest of three men, charging them with stealing her cattle. *The Maitland Mercury* reported that after the men were arrested and their hut searched, a large number of hides had been found with the brands cut out, proving their guilt and fortifying her case against them.

Sadly, this was the beginning of a series of rolling misfortunes for Kelly, and by 1851 she was at war with a number of her neighbours. Often the root of the problem was stock animals – horses, cattle, sheep, pigs – straying onto the other's property, causing damage to crops or gardens or fencing, or just grazing.

The Allan family, who settled at Kimbriki near 'Mount George', were always good friends with Isabella. When they arrived in 1851, their boat was wrecked as it crossed the bar entering the Manning River at Harrington, with only some of their possessions and furniture they had brought with them from England rescued. Isabella graciously offered George and his wife accommodation in her house. The Allan family stayed at 'Mount George' for several months until their own house was built, and Isabella often spent the night with them at Kimbriki.

Late in 1851, Kelly travelled away from 'Mount George' on business, leaving her house locked and unoccupied. When she returned she found it had burnt down, with nothing left but ashes. It was clearly arson as there were no signs of 'natural causes' such as bushfire or lightning strike.

She had lost everything.

More disturbingly for Kelly, apart from the loss of the house itself and the valuable assets it contained, was the issue of who would do such a thing, with little hint as to the identity of the culprit.

Exacerbating her distress was the complete indifference of local Magistrate George Rowley.

The loss of her house led Kelly to take a seven-year lease of a property, 'Brimbin', on the main road from Maitland to Port Macquarie, north of present day Taree and over twenty miles from 'Mount George'. The eight-room house, stockyards and stockmen's huts were in a clearing of dense bush near the river but on ground flat and high enough to be above the general flood level.

On 4 June 1852, thirty-eight-year-old Charles Skerrett, together with wife Maria and their nine children, arrived on horseback at 'Brimbin' to take up residence.

Isabella soon realised the Skerretts were in dire financial straits and helped them as much as possible. On 14 June, Skerrett asked Isabella if he could muster her horses, something she agreed to, offering him a pony and horse as payment, but stating he was only to muster them, not break them in.

Little did she know that she was getting involved with a 'scoundrel' who would cause her much grief in the years to come.

A minor incident occurred not long after, without warning or any real evidence, when on 21 June Isabella was arrested on a charge of cattle stealing. The charge would prove to be vexatious, aimed at the very least to greatly embarrass her, and did not proceed. However, such was a precursor to much more prolonged and vexatious proceedings years later.

On 18 October 1854, Skerrett appeared before Police Magistrate Edward Day and Community Magistrates, James Hawthorne and John Croker, where depositions accusing Skerrett of cattle stealing were read out.

Skerrett offered a simple defence—he *owned* the cattle, producing three documents as proof of his claim:

- A Bill of Sale;
- A Receipt;
- And an agreement signed by Isabella Mary Kelly for Charles Skerrett to muster her horses.

For Isabella, this third document must have come as a tremendous shock. It was genuine, that was difficult to deny, and casting her mind back to various dealings she had had with Skerrett over the years she remembered a situation of her signing the lease of a hut over to him in a document similar to that which he produced to the court—a document she recalled not having fully read over before signing.

William Turner took the witness stand. He had been at' Brimbin' on 6 June and alleged he saw Skerrett give Kelly £400 in four notes, write out the receipt, see Kelly read the receipt and then sign it, with he himself signing the receipt as witness. Magistrate Denny Day adjourned proceedings to 22 November. Skerrett was given bail of £200 with two sureties of £100 each. Day cautioned the public against buying cattle from Charles Skerrett if it contained the brands of Isabella Kelly.

On 5 April 1855, Skerrett stood trial at Central Criminal Court in Darlinghurst for cattle stealing, but there was a complication in the indictment: the verdict rested on whether or not the jury of twelve believed the 'Bill of Sale and Receipt' were forged documents, and yet the charge was for cattle theft, not forgery.

In summing up, Justice Stephen said a great amount of perjury had been presented to the Court by one side or the other throughout the trial. If the prisoner was guilty then he was guilty of infamous fraud and deceit. If he were innocent, the prosecutrix was equally perjured in receiving £400 and depriving the prisoner of his *bona fide* property.

The jury retired and returned twenty minutes later with a verdict of *guilty*, stating their belief that the documents comprising the 'Bill of Sale and Receipt' were forgeries.

Skerrett was gaoled to ten years hard labour on the roads.

With Skerrett in gaol, Isabella Mary Kelly continued her stock operations at 'Brimbin', having resumed her seven-year lease there and at 'Mount George', as well as the A. A. Company lease at 'Mount Gangat'.

On 2 February 1858, with the seven-year lease of 'Brimbin' near its expiration, Kelly bought a 43-acre property, 'Waterview'. There she built a cottage and a stockyard, moving onto the property later in the year. Her horse and cattle operations continued as before, with Isabella moving between the three properties.

Settling into her new property, freed of the drama Skerrett had brought into her life, Kelly may well have thought better times were ahead.

Trouble of one kind or another would, however, continue to haunt Kelly.

In March 1859, a servant girl working for Isabella disappeared from 'Waterview'. This mystery captured the attention and imagination of all the settlers in the Valley, and rumour was rife.

John Allan thought she had gotten lost in the bush, but another settler, Robert Herkes, thought she had been killed, although by whom he could not say.

Henry Flett thought she had eloped with Superintendent Corcoran, who left for New Zealand a short time after the event.

Some said she had been seen in Port Macquarie or along the coast after her disappearance.

Others rumoured that Isabella Kelly killed the girl in a fit of rage.

The mystery was never solved.

Throughout this period, Kelly, now in her late fifties, cast her mind to plans for retirement. She began by selling all her cattle to Cooper & Begbie, a partnership consisting of Maria Cooper and son-in-law Alfred Begbie, who lived at 'Norwood', a few miles upriver from 'Mount George'. Her next step was to sell the sheep and the horses. There were about four hundred horses, but she was experiencing difficulty in selling them at the price she wanted (her prices were, it is said, often rather ambitious and she tended not to sell for less).

The third and final step was to sell 'Mount George', which Isabella decided to break into large farming allotments. The overall plan was to sell everything and in doing so raise about £15000 so Isabella could return home to London to spend her twilight years in the company of friends and relatives of the Crowders, with whom she had remained in regular correspondence during her years away.

A plan, at least for then, is all this remained.

On Saturday 16 July 1859, *The Sydney Morning Herald* reported: 'It perhaps may be in the recollection of many readers that Mr Charles Skerrett some four years ago was, on the information and evidence of Miss Isabella Mary Kelly, tried and convicted on a charge of cattle stealing, and sentenced to ten years' imprisonment. We are now happy to state, on reliable information, that circumstances have lately transpired which have so far proved the innocence of the charge against Mr Skerrett, that the Governor General has been pleased to grant him a complete remission of his sentence.'

Isabella was arrested on Thursday 11 August and given bail. Two days later she appeared at Central Criminal Court for the committal hearing. The Magistrate ruled that a *prima facie* case had been established and committed Kelly to stand trial on the charge of perjury. Bail was set at £500, with two sureties for £250 each.

On Thursday 5 October 1859, the trial of Isabella Mary Kelly began before Mr Justice Dickinson and a jury of four at Darlinghurst. The complexity of the trial came down to this: for the jury to convict Isabella of perjury they would have to decide whether or not the documents were forged. After all the evidence had been presented, the Attorney-General summed up, saying the Chief Justice must have had a valid reason for recommending a free pardon for Skerrett, although Sir Alfred had reported several times he was not in favour of a remission for Skerrett.

However, when he was able to collect new evidence he did recommend the remission and Skerrett was released. If the jury disbelieved Skerrett's story then his two daughters and William Turner were also guilty of perjury.

The main point was whether Kelly had sold her cattle to Skerrett or not, and this was corroborated by the evidence of Philip Dew, Ann Richards, Sam Turner and William Turner.

Mr Justice Dickinson summed up for the jury, taking over two and a half hours.

At nine o'clock the jury of four men retired to consider their verdict. They returned an hour and a quarter later with their verdict: *guilty*.

Isabella was sentenced to twelve months imprisonment and a fine of £100, and was subsequently led away to a damp cell in the adjoining Darlinghurst Gaol. Here she would spend the next six months, albeit with some additional comforts given her station, but imprisoned wrongly nonetheless and determined to be released.

On 6 March 1860, Acting Chief Justice John Dickinson wrote a report to the Governor concerning the case of 'Miss Isabella

Mary Kelly'. A week later, the Governor, Sir William Denison, ordered Kelly's immediate release from gaol —she was pardoned, and to her delight it was a *free* pardon.

As prison officials went to discharge Kelly they found her too ill to be moved and it was not until the next day that she finally left Darlinghurst Gaol.

Describing her departure, Isabella said: 'After the first month [of imprisonment] I never had my health, and when I left I had to be carried out and lifted into the carriage that took me away... one of the women went with me to assist me, for I was not able to sit upright by myself.'

Kelly was taken to Mrs Hoare's boarding house where she would remain for months, very slowly recuperating and unable to exert any real control over her affairs. While in gaol and recovering in Sydney, Kelly failed to pay her rent for the 'Mount Gangat' lease – a matter Lennon & Cape, or their manager Girard, should have remedied.

The A. A. Company went to the Bench for seizure of Kelly's assets to cover the debt. A bailiff, so empowered, seized forty of her horses and then sold them at 'Mount George' for extremely cheap prices.

On 22 October 1861, the Rev Dr John Dunmore Lang, Member for West Sydney, presented a petition to the Legislative Assembly bearing the signatures of 372 persons who were the 'Inhabitants of the Manning River and vicinity', containing the statements:

'And whereas Isabella Mary Kelly has been subjected to much injury and annoyance – pecuniary and otherwise – through loss of property, false imprison and loss of character; Your Petitioners humbly implore that your Honourable House will cause an enquiry to be made into this case, to the end that the ownership of the property may be finally settled, and if it be found that the said Isabella Mary Kelly is the rightful possessor, that a sufficient recompense may be made to her for the injuries she had sustained by loss of property, character, and false imprisonment, and by which she has been reduced to penury.'

On 6 December 1861, David Buchanan, the Member for Morpeth, presented a personal petition from Kelly to the House, detailing the circumstances of the Kelly/Skerrett case and seeking redress for her imprisonment, as well as protection from any potential Skerrett raids on her existing assets.

Following many months of collecting evidence about her case, the final meeting of the Select Committee was held on Tuesday 16 December, but only four members attended – Allen, Flett, Harpur and Stewart. Chairman Allen produced a draft report, which he had written, and asked the Committee to read it. The Report valued Miss Kelly's assets at the time of Skerrett's release at £10,350, with no consideration given to her Maitland properties as they did not sustain losses.

The Committee formed three main opinions:

- The documents of 'Bill of Sale and Receipt' were forgeries;
- Their loss before Kelly's trial had seriously prejudiced her defence;
- Sir Alfred, in giving his evidence at the trial, had misled the jury.

The Committee recommended the House accept Isabella had a valid claim to compensation, and in deciding how much compensation she should be awarded, the House should take into consideration:

- The money she had lost as a result of her unjust conviction;
- Her loss of health and liberty;
- The injury sustained to her reputation.

Sadly, this was where Kelly's past would come back to haunt her.

Flett, that spurned suitor from so long ago, decided his cold dish of revenge was ready to be served, moving a motion to appoint a third select committee to look at fresh evidence on the grounds that the sum of money was too large not to ensure all evidence had been collected, a motion carried by the House.

This was an unprecedented third Select Committee to enquire into these same matters – the Skerrett Select Committee of 1860, the Kelly Select Committee of 1862 and now the Kelly Select Committee of 1863.

Thomas Garrett, Member for Monaro, joined the new Select Committee at their first meeting, two days later under the chairmanship of William Allen. Garrett was a youthful thirty-two years of age, and at the start of a long and distinguished political career. Flett and Garrett were friends, and whenever they were in Sydney for Parliamentary sessions would take lodgings together. Having been nominated by Flett, Garrett would completely support Flett, both in the questioning of witnesses before the 1863 Committee and in the voting. He seemed to genuinely believe whatever Flett told him about Isabella.

Not only did Henry Flett now have an ally on the Committee, but the witnesses called by him to attend this third enquiry would all be hostile to Isabella. This Report was very similar to the 1862 Report, but it now spoke of 'the improbability of Miss

Kelly having made the lease' with Richards before.

It found that:

- The 'Bill of Sale and Receipt' documents were forgeries;
- Miss Kelly was wrongfully convicted of having committed perjury;
- The Chief Justice mislaid the 'Bill of Sale and Receipt', and in consequence her defence was seriously prejudiced;
- Miss Kelly was in prison more than five months, and her health and constitution suffered severely.

On 20 October 1863, William Allen presented the nine-page Report to the House of Assembly, including the transcripts of their interviews and the many appendices. The House ordered the Report to be printed. Twelve months after the report of the 1863 Select Committee had been presented to the House there was still no sign of compensation for Kelly coming before the House—the report gathered dust on a shelf.

On 5 May 1865, eighteen months after the House had first failed to debate the Select Committee's Report, the Rev. Dr John Dunmore Lang rose in the Legislative Assembly and moved that the House go into a Committee of the Whole to consider the Report of the Select Committee on the Petition of Isabella Mary Kelly.

Dr Lang and Isabella had first met thirty years previously as fellow cabin passengers on board the *James*, and Lang had presented her first petition to Parliament. Many would regard this as a rather incongruous pairing – a single Catholic lady and a militant Presbyterian Minister, not averse to anti-Catholic sentiment on occasion.

In speaking to his motion, Dr Lang said he had been asked by certain Members of the House to defer his motion, but the 'Lady', who was the subject of his motion, moved in a very respectable class of society and had been possessed of a large amount of property. Miss Kelly had been deprived of her property and imprisoned on a charge of perjury, of which she was altogether innocent. He hoped that the Members would not be so ungallant as to postpone this matter any further.

The House passed his motion and moved into committee mode.

Dr Lang outlined the history of the case from Isabella's arrival in the colony as a woman of wealth to her conviction for perjury and eventual release from prison, but it was John Darvall, Isabella's former defence barrister, who made the decisive speech. Nothing, he declared, could truly compensate for her loss of property and health. These losses had occurred through a most unhappy miscarriage of justice. His main line was that she deserved some monetary compensation and he would suggest to the House that £1,000 be inserted into Dr Lang's motion.

'Hear, hear' apparently resounded around the Chamber – £1,000, although large, was an amount that most Members could accept as an adequate cost of concluding the matter.

Having been awarded the compensation by the government, Isabella made preparations to return to England. On 11 September 1865, she sold 'Waterview' for £45, ending twenty-seven years of residence in the Manning Valley, and just over a month later, on 17 October, Isabella received £250 of the £1,000 compensation.

Not long after she slipped out of Sydney and travelled to Melbourne, the main Australian terminal in that period for England-Australia shipping, finally departing for London in December.

The last years of the life of Isabella Mary Kelly are as full of mystery as her early years, with little recorded of her time spent back in London.

Her writings do, however, reflect a deep sadness displayed by Isabella as she put to paper her feelings about her return to England after an absence of thirty years.

'Strange to say that nearly all my friends are dead. There are only two families left out of the many that I knew before I left England for Australia. My friends the Crowder family are all dead, but four. Mrs Crowder made me a present of a very handsome gold watch which belonged to [her husband] the late Sir Richard Crowder. I was invited to Reeding for a few weeks... To see the style and grandeur that they live in is remarkable – coachmen, butlers, and footmen.'

Too much had changed and too much had happened in her life in the intervening years since her departure three decades earlier.

Simply put, England was no longer home.

Isabella returned to Sydney sometime during the period 1868–70.

On May 16, 1871, John Dillon, the twenty-four year old Member for Hunter, rose in the House of Assembly and moved that 'a sum not exceeding £1,000, to supplement a sum previously voted [six years ago] by this House as compensation to Miss Isabella Mary Kelly, for her unjust incarceration in one of her Majesty's gaols of this colony' be awarded to Isabella.

The motion was defeated nineteen votes to nine.

Thirteen months later, Isabella Mary Kelly died.

The death certificate recorded her passing away on 24 June 1872 from a 'decay of nature' with the duration of the illness noted as 'some time'.

Maybe it should have rightly read 'she died of a broken spirit', having never fully recovered from the years of trouble Skerrett and others had brought upon her...

Georgiana Molloy

1805-1867

As the industrial revolution rolled across Europe, bringing with it a vast array of technologies never seen before that would forever change the ways we live our lives, it was men, more often than not, than women who were the beneficiaries of this revolution.

And it was men in the 'professions' in particular who were most able to take advantage of this 'revolution' to build their wealth and esteem.

Of course, the idea of women holding professional roles in society was mostly non-existent. For the most, at least, they remained dutifully bound to fulfilling their roles as wives, mothers and homemakers, with little thought of having something resembling a professional life, except maybe amongst the very wealthy.

And yet some women, even in the most subtle and unintended

ways, helped begin a long-overdue, if still rather slow, turning of the vast cogs and wheels of social change that would in time begin the propulsion of women more generally into a position where they could hold their own professionally against men, if not prove their sex the better.

ONE OF A FAMILY of five children born to David and Mary Kennedy, Georgiana Kennedy entered this world not long after the turn of the century in Cumberland in the north of England in 1805.

She grew up in some degree of comfort and privilege, but following the death of her father, the family dissolved into a state of disarray. Her mother was deep in mourning at the loss of her husband and there was some fractious squabbling between Georgiana and her siblings, Elizabeth, Mary, Daltron and George.

To escape this unhappy environment, Georgiana relocated to Scotland where close family friend, the Dunlops, opened their welcoming arms and home to her. This move was also prompted by her connection to the Christian Revival Movement, with which Georgiana had become fervently involved and that would remain a major part of her beliefs for the rest of her life.

It was there, in Scotland, that she met Captain John Molloy.

John was a striking-looking seafarer, the illegitimate son of the Duke of York—the brother of King George II—and almost double Georgiana's age. This did not prevent the pair falling hopelessly in love, with the twenty-four-year old Georgiana and forty-eight-year old John becoming betrothed on the 1 August 1829.

Wasting no time, a day later Georgiana moved to Glasgow to begin preparations for the journey of a lifetime: to the new colony, Australia.

By October, with eight servants in tow and all their household possessions packed into crates, the Molloys were aboard *The Warrior*, Western Australia-bound. The journey would take six months and was not without hardship as a pregnant Georgiana suffered the dreaded *mal de mer*, but remained fortified by her adoring and attentive husband.

They arrived at the Swan River outpost (later Perth) in March 1830, and one can but imagine Georgiana's state of shock upon stepping foot off *The Warrior* and being immediately presented with such a completely alien environment so far away from home.

A relentless sun, the rays of which seemed to beat down with an intense heat never before experienced or imagined in the cool climes of her birthplace.

A landscape filled with flora and fauna of exotic shape and colour and form she had not believed possible.

And, besides the limited personal possessions that had come with them, nothing more in the way of more extensive furnishings or creature comforts to help recreate in some fashion the contented life she had once known.

What outlandish world had she had allowed herself to be brought to?!

Six weeks after their arrival, the shock of the new settling in to some degree, the Molloys set forth to travel further afield to the mouth of the Blackwood River on Flinders Bay (where Augusta lies today), a region that remained vastly unexplored.

Accompanying the official party of Governor Stirling, the man who had effectively established and now governed Swan River, with two other families in tow (one being the Bussells, who would themselves become a much-renowned Western Australian clan) they trekked 300km through the late autumn until they arrived in the heavily-timbered country of the proposed sub-colony.

Not long after, Georgiana gave birth to their first child.

Sadly, this child was not meant to be, the infant dying just a few days later, maybe not entirely unsurprising after the hardships of the long journey since leaving Scotland and the lack of facilities at hand to help with the birth.

Georgiana recovered from the death, yet remained deeply depressed at the loss. Over time, she came to herself once more, and despite the ever-challenging conditions began the task of creating a home.

The small community bravely struggled tried to establish itself, going without many of the basic necessities. Supplies could take months to reach them, the land remained harsh and unforgiving, and relations with the local indigenous population were strained. Georgiana faced the added burden of Jack often being absent, travelling the country in his capacity as a Resident Magistrate, leaving her in charge of attending to the household and bringing up the two children to whom she had since given birth.

Diaries she kept at the time unsurprisingly indicate a deep unhappiness and desire to return to England, but this was clearly out of the question, so Georgiana committed herself as much as she was able to the life before her.

Of some relief were the books of literature and poetry she had originally brought with her and that also sometimes arrived with the infrequent supply carts from Swan River. These at least gave her some intellectual occupation to help fill the lonely periods when Jack was away performing his duties.

She also began to garden once more.

A keen gardener back home in England, with time at last on her hands Georgiana saw no reason why she should not take up this enjoyable and once rewarding pastime. Having brought with her from England some tools and a variety of seeds, even in an environment of which she still had little understanding in terms of fertility, climate and other planting considerations, her green thumb rose to the fore and she did what she could with what she had.

After experiencing some difficulties, and with only mixed success attempting to grow her beloved and familiar English varieties, she took a new tack. Rather than 'garden' in the more conventional sense, Georgiana began to observe and take note of the indigenous plants that flourished around her, gathering, pressing and mounting them in something resembling a *horticus siccus*—a botanist's herbarium.

Word of her amateur botanical pursuits got back to the wife of Governor Stirling, who in turn contacted her cousin in England, Captain James Mangles. Mangles was himself an amateur botanist who was fascinated by the news and excited at the prospects of making contact with Georgiana, seeing it as a wonderful opportunity to have someone 'on the ground' in the colonies with access to all manner of native species.

Over some correspondence he struck up a relationship with Georgiana.

In December 1836, he sent her a box of English seeds in what he hoped was fair exchange for the return to him of local specimens. In his letter he urged her to send him samples and seeds of natives of the region, which he then intended supplying to various organisations and collectors in England eager for cuttings from the colonies.

Georgiana took up his request with zeal.

Sending off her first 'shipment', Mangles immediately noted how meticulous her methods of collection and preservation were.

She not only carefully prepared the specimens, but went much further, providing a plethora of information about each species, gathered either from her own observations or from information she gleaned from local friendly indigenous people.

As Mangles passed on her seeds to other horticulturalists and botanists in England, word spread about her botanical activities and more people became interested in her, with several having great success in cultivating Australian species on English soil from the specimens prepared and shipped to Mangles by Molloy.

When in 1839 the family moved 100kms north to the Vasse district in hope of finding land easier to develop, she continued her 'work' even as they went about the task of building a new homestead, 'FairLawn', and despite her having another child on the way born not long after their move.

In 1839 and 1842 botanists visited Georgiana, adding yet another level of gravitas to the work she was doing. Her enthusiasm for these botanical pursuits fed a desire to extend her knowledge in the field, which she did from both books sent by Mangles, and by utilising the knowledge of the region's flora and fauna provided by another local indigenous tribe with whom she made contact.

For seven years the exchanges with Mangles continued.

As part of these he sent gifts for her and the children, and their relationship extended beyond that of 'botanical colleagues'...they also became good friends. She wrote him long letters, sent along with her shipments, and clearly enough of a degree of intimacy developed between them for her to discuss the intense grief she felt after her nineteen-month son accidentally drowned in a well in 1838.

This working relationship and friendship may have continued for many more years were it not for Georgiana's failing constitution. Bouts of ill health that plagued her after each of her pregnancies (she bore seven children over twelve years) were slowly causing a more general deterioration of her wellbeing.

Her body had had enough.

The birth of one daughter, then another, gradually wore her down to the point of no return. Following the birth of her fifth daughter, she fell seriously ill and never really recovered. Her body continued to haemorrhage blood in far more dramatic fashion than it had following earlier pregnancies and the prognosis looked poor.

Yet although Georgiana remained effectively bed-bound, her fervour to continue the botanical pursuits, such an important part of her life, remained. With the help of her daughters, who she would send out with strict instructions in terms of the collection of specimens, she was able to keep up her end of the bargain as she continued to collect seeds for Mangles and prepare them with all her usual professional efficiency.

In this way she would continue the work she loved right up until the time her compromised health would fail her permanently.

Just three months after the birth of her last child, named Georgiana after herself, Georgiana's body could sustain her no longer and she died on 8 April 1843.

At the still-young age of just thirty-seven she had lived a full life and achieved so much—much more than she might ever have imagined those fifteen years before when she first set off into the unknown alongside her beloved John.

Her passing did not go un-noted.

George Hailes, a horticulturalist who knew of her and had benefitted much from her work, proclaimed her valuable contribution to botany, saying 'Not one in ten thousand who go out into distant lands has done what she did for the Gardens of her Native Country...'

Even in death, she had left a lasting, ongoing legacy from her years of enjoyable toil.

John Molloy remained at the settlement after her death, going on to live another twenty years before being finally being buried alongside his beloved and most talented wife in October 1867.

Despite only receiving minor accolades for her important work, Georgiana Molloy remains a woman who made a valuable contribution in educating those half a world away about the botanical nature of the new colony.

And perhaps, more subtly, yet just as importantly, she was also part of the early whisperings of a movement where women would begin to launch themselves into as yet uncharted territory: a world where females were capable of having professional lives to match that of their male counterparts.

Emma Mary Withnell

1842-1928

'The Mother of the North West' is a grand-sounding title.

Such is attributed to a pioneering woman who defied her father's wishes to take up with the man she loved, and head far from him in the hope of material success at a time when Western Australia was still very much a rough and tumble frontier of Australia's slowly evolving nation.

This 'mother' would find great challenges before her 'out west' that would challenge her and require her to draw deeply upon her maternal instincts to help both her own family and others in need.

ESTERN AUSTRALIA OF 1842 was the westernmost fledgling frontline of the new colony. Settlements were slow
to grow. Swan River had a population of less than 1500 and the
remainder of the West's population, as small as it was, had concentrated on the south-western coastline at Bunbury, Augusta
and Albany.

Sheep farmers were slowly making inroads in settling the West,
with notable success in the Avon Valley in the 1830s, and ventures
spreading further afield to the Pilbara in the 1860s and beyond.

On 19 December 1842, a Guildford farmer, George Hancock
and his wife Sophia, both of whom had arrived in Fremantle
from London aboard *the Warrior* in 1830 (coincidentally the same
vessel Georgiana Molloy also voyaged to Australia on), were
blessed with the birth of a daughter, Emma Mary, who would be
one of seven female children the family would eventually come
to comprise.

Emma's upbringing was farm-based, with her father educating
her on site, something she would later replicate with the eleven
children she would go on to bear and need to similarly educate.

Taking up the opportunity for a bigger property in the York
district, the family moved and had some more success there.
Emma, by this time growing well into womanhood, gained the
attention of neighbouring pastoralist, John Withnell.

As the pair became acquainted, and their attraction for one
another grew, a short courtship ensued, with John going on to ask
for her hand in marriage. Prospective father-in-law George was
initially against the union, concerned for his daughter's welfare
in taking up with a none-too-well-off Withnell. Understandably,
he wanted the best for his child, and proved stubborn over the

matter until Emma herself had 'words' with him.

The ever-practical, intelligent and strong-willed daughter remarked to her recalcitrant father, 'When you have seven daughters, and they are all as plain as me, you should be grateful for an honest man, even if he is poor, to take one of them off your hands.'[1]

After a little more 'discussion', Emma had her way and took the name Withnell on 10 May 1859.

For the next five years, she and her husband strived to make a profitable go at the land John held, but had only marginal success. As much as it might have pained Emma to admit, it seemed on some level that her father had been correct in his summation of Withnell.

She was, however, a stubborn and resilient woman.

Determined not to be proven wrong in her choice of partner, upon hearing word from a cousin that the north-west of the state, the Pilbara, was opening up as a potentially profitable new district for grazing, Emma encouraged John to consider heading there to see what they could make of it.

Encouraged by his wife's support, John agreed, and in March 1864, with two young children, Emma's sister, Fanny, and all their livestock, the family set forth in the direction of the DeGrey River aboard a chartered boat, *the Sea Ripple*, with hopes of a new life in the area of Port Hedland.

The gentle name of the schooner might have served as a hopeful premonition of the journey ahead, but regrettably proved the opposite.

---

1 http://pandora.nla.gov.au/pan/95993/20090319-1853/now
andthen.noadsfree.com/withnell.html

Approaching their destination, a violent storm drove the ship ashore, badly breached as it hit banks of rocks on the way. The humans aboard escaped with their lives, but the precious livestock that was to be the Withnells new hope suffered greatly. Though they took as much care as possible when unloading the stock, in the stormy conditions many of the sheep were lost, leaving them with a much-reduced flock of sixty or so.

Not to be deterred, they patched up *the Sea Ripple* as best they could and managed to limp across calmer waters to Tien Tsin Harbour (about 200km south-west of where Port Hedland is located today) where the tiny community of Cossack lay at Nickol Bay.

Upon landing, after a swift settling-in period, and despite the large loss of their prospective livelihood and many of their possessions, the Withnells began scouring the locale for a place to call home. Guided by the need to be near a source of freshwater, they headed inland and eventually set up camp on the Harding River, where not long after Emma gave birth to child number three.

Following the birth, the first and most important challenge was the building of a suitable dwelling to call home, something the family began to construct immediately, establishing their first homestead on 30,000ha at 'Mount Welcome Station', and also taking up another 100,000ha at 'Sherlock Station'.

There was also the financial imperative to begin taking advantage of the small herd that had survived the arduous trip. They commenced shearing in September of that same year and worked on a breeding programme to grow the herd back to its numbers prior to the loss they experienced during their traumatic arrival in the region.

As part of this, like many other settlers, they recruited the help of local indigenous men as shepherds, shearers and general labourers, with the women employed to assist in the running of the Mount Welcome homestead.

For all their efforts, the return, sadly, was minimal, and both John and Mary became concerned about their financial straits.

Action needed to be taken.

Leaving Emma to run the station, John headed to Nickol Bay. The fledgling pearling industry, originally successfully established at Shark Bay, had set up operations there and John took to it in the hope of making his fortune. Emma, meantime, did all she could to keep her family safe, educated and fed, while running the station to the best of her ability.

It was a lonely, isolated existence, even with her children and sister present, but she managed, ever hoping for better times. Although initially wary of local indigenous tribes, especially being sole protector of her family in the absence of John, as she employed more of the locals around the station, Emma slowly dropped her guard and established congenial relationships. This led to a period where she became trusted and respected as 'a medicine woman' when nursing and vaccinating many of the local indigenous population during a smallpox epidemic in 1866.

This level of respect for both her and John grew so great that they were named a 'Boorang' and a 'Banaker', titles of esteem that allowed them to move freely amongst the tribes.

During this period, surveyors began assessing the locale for the establishment of a new town to be titled Roeburne. 'Mount Welcome', being so close to fresh water and already something of a hub for the local community, was placed right in the middle of the most suitable land, and as a consequence the Withnells were offered prime real estate within the environs of the proposed town. To compensate them for the loss of their larger property, they also received holdings out on the Sherlock River.

Throwing in the pearling, John saw the establishment of the town as an opportunity to be more permanently with his family. Realising that some kind of transportation would be required to move both people and stock to the ocean, he started a ferry service, and when not ferrying people or items, worked as the local butcher.

However, bad luck was once more to plague Emma and her hardy pioneering clan.

In 1867, the supply ship *Emma* (named after Emma herself) foundered in bad weather, bringing more financial loss to the Withnells. Not only did they lose money from this tragedy, but also much produce and some dear friends who resided in the area.

The years that followed would bring no easing of their bad luck.

First, there were a series of droughts that severely compromised their livestock business.

Then, in 1872, a devastating cyclone wreaked further havoc, killing many of their livestock and destroying the homestead. In true pioneering spirit, they rebuilt, only to have their hard work once more torn asunder in 1878 when a fire ripped through the property. The blaze destroyed most of the buildings and left the Whitnells to seriously ponder what to do next—rebuild, or move on, once again, and try their luck in some other locale?

These unfortunate occurrences, and the fact that Roeburne was steadily growing to the point that it was now too big to still be the peaceful environs Emma and John had helped established, prompted the couple to move to one of their outlying holdings on the Sherlock River. There they lived in relative peace, albeit of the hard working kind, for nearly a decade during a period that marked a welcome respite from the spate of bad luck that had seemed to haunt them for so long.

As the Withnells grew older and began to consider their retirement, their sons were now in the financial position of being able to take over the running of the holding. One of them, Jimmy, would gain some fame as the first man to discover gold-bearing rock in the Pilbara, which would lead not long after to the launching of the rich Pilbara goldfields.

Approaching the age of fifty, and after so many struggles and the birth of eleven children, it was at last time for a more relaxed existence for Emma and the man she had stuck by through all manner of life events. In 1888, the couple travelled back to Guildford, where they had met so many years before, and settled into retirement, which would continue for a decade until John's death in 1898.

Following his death, Emma, still in relatively good health considering the number of children she had borne and the rugged existence she had lived, would spend the next thirty years between Northam, where she took up residence, and the homes of her assorted children in and around Perth. During this time she became Western Australia's first female Justice of the Peace while retaining some interest in the far northwest after purchasing an interest in 'Karratha Station'.

At the venerable age of eighty-six, in May 1928 Emma was struck down with cholecystitis while visiting one of her sons at

Mt Lawley, dying not long after. She was buried in the Guildford cemetery, ending a long life filled with much hardship and yet, through it all, much joy and love.

Today, the 'Mother of the north-west' is fondly remembered as one of the great pioneering outback women of Western Australia, with a portrait of her hanging proudly in the 'Hall of Pioneer's' at the National Trust property at Mangowine.

Emma Withnell's name is also commemorated around the state, enshrined in the titles of parks, streets and landmarks; marks of respect for this wonderful woman and important reminders that resilience, determination and courage, with equal measures of love and compassion, are the key ingredients for survival when one is up against so many obstacles and challenges beyond one's control.

Grace Drake-Brockmann (nee Russell)

1860-1935

The sea, at its most cruel and violent, takes no prisoners...only lives.

Over the centuries we have traversed the nautical highways, many souls have perished in the hungry maw of one ocean or another, often the victims of man's own folly for thinking he is invincible when it comes to untameable Mother Nature.

In 1545, *The Mary Rose* heeled over in squally winds, capsizing and taking all but 70 of her men with her.

The Lusitania sank in 1915 when torpedoed by the German navy, with over 1200 sinking to their watery graves.

A Swedish freight-ship collided with the *Andrea Doria* in 1956, although loss of life was kept to just 54.

And of course there was 'that' iceberg and that ship that 'God himself couldn't sink'…apparently…but did, with a '*Titanic*' 1503 passengers lost.

Luckily, not all shipwrecks have such tragic finales.

And thanks to the bravery and courage of one of our outback heroines, the *S.S. Georgette* is one of them.

FOLLOWING THE DEATH OF their clergyman father, in 1829 the Bussell brothers made a somewhat dramatic, yet momentous decision—to immigrate to the colonies to the new frontier of Western Australia.

Arriving at the Swan River colony, they found it in the midst of the throes of establishing itself as the first major outpost on the Western side of the continent, and 'out there', in all that land and space, there awaited who-knew-what incredible opportunities for willing and brave men like the Bussells.

The Bussell boys—Alfred, John, Charles, Lennox and Vernon—took up the challenge, heading south to Augusta on the Blackwood River with an official expedition backed by Governor Stirling.

Their mission?

To start a sub-colony with another pioneering family...the Molloys, as fate would have it.

Finding the land not to their liking due to its limited viability for farming, they moved on to Adelphi, but after being burnt out there went on to settle in Vasse. This area seemed a more likely prospect than any of the places they had come across so far for the founding of a rural community that could support itself and commence financially-viable agricultural operations.

So, finally established, the Bussell boys' mother and sisters made the journey from England to join them.

Alfred Bussell met a local woman, Ellen Heppingstone, who he courted then married. Initially, they moved to a pro-perty, 'Ellensbrook', where they sought to create a dairy and cattle farm. However, after it was burnt out in 1856, the Bussells moved on to the mouth of the Margaret River to a 24,000ha property, 'Wallcliffe'.

A few years later in 1860, a daughter, Grace, was born to them.

The children of the Bussell household, like the children of so many other pioneering families, spent their childhoods predominantly on the farm, helping out with the daily chores. Grace was also a keen horse-rider, and something of an adventurer and explorer, allegedly discovering at the age of ten 'Wallcliffe Cave' just behind her home in 1870, and another, 'Calgardup Cave', in 1878.

An event far more significant, however, would occur in the time between these two 'discoveries', propelling Grace into the heart of a far more historic 'adventure'.

One that would make her a heroine.

On 29 November 1876, the combination steam and sail schooner *S.S. Georgette* departed Fremantle. She was bound for Adelaide, via Bunbury, Busselton and Albany, laden with a cargo of Jarrah, the hardwood native of the region, assorted supplies and a group of 50 passengers.

As they departed, little did the captain, crew and passengers know *The Georgette* was heading into troubled waters.

Two days later, some 32kms out to sea, in the thick of night just after 'twelve bells', *The Georgette* began taking on water. Whether this breach originated from some kind of damage done to the ship while its cargo was loaded, or was in fact a longstanding weakness in the bough, the leak quickly turned into a much more serious problem.

By 4am, frantic attempts at trying to get the pumps working were abandoned. In an attempt to save the stricken vessel, all hands, including as many passengers as were physically able, were called upon to man themselves with buckets in an effort to remove the flood of water gushing into the bough.

Their efforts, though tireless, were in vain as water kept pouring in through the breach faster than they could bucket it out, and the time came to take the only other option: prepare the lifeboats to abandon ship.

The first over the side, filled with 20 passengers, was almost immediately destroyed as it smashed against the hull, scattering its terrified human contents into the boiling, angry ocean. Two women and five children were lost, the rest retrieved by the second lifeboat, which attempted to make the arduous trip ashore.

In the meantime, those remaining on board went back to their seemingly useless attempts at saving the SS *Georgette*. Two hours later, still bailing, their toil came to naught as the boiler room flooded and the ship remained adrift somewhere in the vicinity just a few kilometres north of the mouth of the Margaret River. Assessing the situation as hopeless, the crew immediately ran the ship under sail to the coast, grounding her in Calgardup Bay, south of Prevelly, where she began the slow torturous process of breaking up.

Sam Isaacs, an indigenous stockman employed by the Bussells, was out on his rounds that morning. From the shore, even at such a distance he was able to comprehend this unfolding tragedy, so Isaacs mounted his horse and rode the 20-odd kilometres back to the property for help.

At such an early hour, he was surprised to find Grace already awake, helping her mother bake the day's bread.

What could the young girl be doing up so early?

The sixteen-year-old had awoken from a bad dream, one of

a string of recurring nightmares in which she found herself riding a horse along a beach. Seeing a ship in trouble with people drowning in the surf, she would race to the aid of these doomed souls and rescue them. The dream that particular morning had been so vivid that she had been unable to shake it off and return to sleep, so, wide-awake, she had headed to the kitchen and her mother.

Sam immediately delivered the terrible news to them, and suddenly, it seemed, in some prophetic way, Grace's dreams were coming true.

A more delicate 'gal' than Grace might have stumbled at this revelation, especially given its seemingly direct correlation to her recent dreams.

But not Grace.

Rather than be spooked by this incredible coincidence, she immediately dropped what she was doing and jumped into action. Collecting ropes with Sam, they saddled up their horses and galloped off, covering the distance at breakneck speed as they pushed their horses, knowing time was of the essence if they were to be of any assistance in salvaging whatever passengers might be left on the foundering vessel.

Arriving at the site of the wreck, Grace raced down from the cliff-top and across the dunes, fearlessly pounding straight into the surf. She swam her horse out through the breakers until she reached a lifeboat, where she began urging those wretched souls she found adrift to grab hold wherever they could, then began hauling them back to the shore.

This initial brave act was just the beginning of a day of heroism. No sooner had she deposited her first batch of survivors upon the shore than she was off again, turning her stead back out into the water where more remained in need of rescue. Sam, following her example, began making similar trips out into the water, and between them they brought in every soul possible.

Capping off her already extraordinary acts of courage, Grace, seeing some passengers still clinging to the stranded ship, took her now tiring horse out as far as the foundering vessel itself, encouraging people to jump out to her and the horse so they could be led to the shore.

After four hours of this arduous labour, Grace and Sam surveyed the fruits of their efforts—they had somehow managed to save every remaining man, woman and child.

Although wearied beyond belief, Grace mustered herself and horse to one last effort to ride home and raise help to attend to the bedraggled survivors. Alfred Bussell immediately began to put together a full rescue party, which he sent out to the site of the catastrophe.

The miserable but safe humans were guided slowly back to Wallcliffe House where the Bussells offered them shelter and sustenance.

In the wake of this momentous effort, Grace was hailed a heroine, christened 'The Grace Darling of the West' after an English girl who had performed a similar rescue in 1838. Both she and Sam were awarded medals by the Royal Humane Society of England, although, maybe somewhat unfairly, and as a sign of the poor attitudes towards indigenous people at the time, Grace received a silver medal whereas Sam only received a bronze.

Grace was also awarded a gold watch by the State Government, Sam a parcel of land in recognition of his deeds and her father one hundred pounds by way of compensation for the family's care of the survivors of the wreck.

Not long after, hearing of Grace's bravery, a government surveyor, Frederick Drake Brockmann, rode the 300km from Perth to meet this amazing young woman who people were talking so much about, and upon being introduced, found himself attracted to her.

Friendship turned to courtship, and they went on to marry in 1882 in what would later become the town of Busselton.

Over the next 25 years Frederick's career would advance until he reached the top of his field, becoming the Surveyor General of WA. The couple would produce seven children and Grace would live a long and happy life.

Her famous exploits would lead to the coastal hamlet of Gracetown, north of the Margaret River, being named after her, as well as another town in the wheat-belt, Lake Grace, also named in her honour.

She died in 1935 at the age of 75.

Heroes, or heroines, are defined by the moment in which they make a selfless decision that potentially imperils them, but saves another...or in some cases many others.

In the wake of strangely prophetic dreams, and at the age of just sixteen, without a moment's thought for her own safety, Grace Bussell inadvertently entered the 'hall of heroic deeds' as she unselfishly saved the lives of men, women and children who were nothing to her as complete strangers, yet everything to her as humans in dire need.

The plaque that stands today at Redgate Beach, not far from the site of the wreck of *The Georgette*, remains a lasting testament to this heroism—a reminder to us all of how we can stand up to even the wild whims of nature herself and deliver life from the jaws of seemingly certain death.

Famous Early Amazonian Writers

19th-20th century

*Women, then, have not had a dog's chance
of writing poetry.
That is why I have laid so much stress on money
and a room of one's own.*

Virginia Woolf, *A Room of One's Own*

As Australia began to articulate its own identity, it was only natural that a collection of literature should also begin to develop as a method of recording and illustrating the emerging nation.

Adam Lindsay Gordon.
Banjo Patterson.
Henry Handel Richardson.

All familiar and famous literary *men* of the time—but what of the women?

Once again, just as with their colonial forebears, they were present, documenting their experiences and also writing more creatively, desirous of adding to our nation's growing body of literary works.

Such women would make astute and detailed observations of Australian life and the life, in particular, of its indigenous peoples, painstakingly recording such, and their work would not only go on to entertain and inform generations of Australian, but would also add to a more serious body of research, particularly in the area of indigenous peoples.

Daisy Bates

1859-1951

*I have tried to tell of their being and their
ending and the cause of their decline.
Nothing is ever lost in this world,
and if the slightest impression of anything I have
said or done, by example or in devotion, remains with
them in comfort for the past or hope for the future,
I shall be content.*

Daisy Bates, *The Passing of the Aborigines*

The term 'Kabbarli' is an honour rarely bestowed upon a non-indigenous female.

And yet a white woman, who did almost all in her power to connect with Australia's native population, was the proud recipient of the title, which translates as 'grandmotherly person'.

Despite some controversy at the time surrounding components of her documented beliefs concerning the long-term future of indigenous Australians, she carried the title to her grave and is referred to it even today.

This same woman would also have a reputation as being extremely curious and highly intelligent. She was also romantically linked, possibly even married, to more than one man at a time.

In many ways she was a 'modern' woman before her time, not to be framed as a helpless appendage to males, instead having a strong will, never-say-die attitude and lifestyle of her own choosing rather than that of her husband, unlike so many of her peers at the time.

THE ROLLING GREEN HILLS of Tipperary are a far cry from the harsh dry heat and scorched conditions of outback Australia, but it was there in October 1859[2] that shopkeepers James and Marguarette Dwyer were blessed with the coming of a baby daughter, Margaret May.

The young girl would know little of her mother, who contracted tuberculosis and died just a handful of years later. Suddenly presented with a life absent of maternal love and support, this must have been a bewildering loss for the four-year-old Margaret.

Adding to this instability, although not intentionally as it is likely he was hoping to fill the hole left by the loss of Margaret's mother, James remarried. This new union was to be short-lived, however, as he passed away not long after on-board a ship to the United States of America.

Now a complete orphan, Margaret was taken under the wing of her widowed grandmother at Ballyrcrine, happy for the chance to live with her until the elderly woman passed away, at which point Margaret's life was once again thrown into turmoil as the property she lived in was sold, leaving her now without kin or home.

Yet another death in the family for the eight-year-old meant far greater geographical upheaval, this time further afield to London where, via an English Charitable Organisation, she was placed in the household of Sir Francis Outram as his ward.

Under his care, she was educated and maintained until her early teens, at which point she returned to Rosecrea to live with her uncle Joe. There, the Sisters of the Sacred Heart of Mary offered

---

2 Daisy herself claimed she was born in 1863, which it is believed she did to conceal her first marriage

her further schooling until around the age of twenty, training her in the 'respectable' profession of becoming a governess.

A certain degree of mystery obfuscates the next portion of Margaret's life and the circumstances surrounding her departure from home in 1882 to take up the opportunity of a £1 assisted immigrant voyage to Queensland, Australia.

Comments in her own diaries indicate that a milder version of the disease that had killed her mother returned to plague Margaret herself. Apparently suffering from pulmonary tuberculosis, in November 1882 she embarked for the colonies aboard the *R.M.S. Almora* as a means of recovering her health and starting afresh.

And for reasons one can only guess at, sometime during the journey 'Margaret' changed her name to 'Daisy May O'Dwyer'.

This change of name raises questions as to the real reason for Margaret/Daisy's departure from England. It could be that it was a metaphorical statement in that she wished to wipe the slate clear—a new name to go with the new life in Australia.

Or possibly she met someone on-board *the Almora* who inspired her to change her name to something more befitting of her new home.

Or maybe it was just simply that she had always hated the name Margaret!

There are, however hints at possibly a more sinister reason for the change.

In a biography on Bates written by Julia Blackburn, *Daisy Bates in the Desert: A Woman's Life Among the Aborigines*, a slightly more ominous account is suggested as to both Margaret/Daisy's leaving (or possibly fleeing) England and the name change that accompanied this.

Blackburn indicates that sometime after Bates took up a role as a governess in Dublin at the age of eighteen, there was some kind of scandal, possibly of sexual nature, that tragically ended in someone from the household she was employed at taking his life. The details of this are sketchy, and even if the suicide did occur, whether or not Bates was somehow involved remains conjecture.

However, following this line of reasoning one can imagine that a fearful Bates, needing to escape this unsavoury situation, fled the household and Ireland itself. Margaret Dwyer transformed into Daisy May O'Dwyer, removing herself both identity-wise and as geographically far as possible from the alleged scandal.

Perhaps the truth will never be known, but, for whatever reason in January 1883 it was 'Daisy May O'Dwyer' who walked down the gangplank of *The Almora* in Townsville, Queensland, and this would be the name Margaret Dwyer would take to her grave many years later.

After a long sea voyage she would later paint as an enjoyable pleasure cruise (which, given the state of sea travel at the time, is more likely a creative version of the reality of the actual journey), Daisy secured herself a position as governess with a Charters Towers pastoralist at the 'Fanning Downs Station'.

Here, she would meet her first of several husbands, a poet and horseman, called Edwin Murrant, in March 1884.

At first, this name may not sound overly familiar, but according to biographer Nick Bleszynski, Daisy convinced Edwin to transform his surname to one that would later become indelibly imprinted on the Australian psyche—Harry Harbord 'Morant'.

The very same 'Breaker' Morant who would be court-marshalled and consequently put to death by firing squad for his alleged involvement in the deaths of surrendering enemy soldiers while he was posted in Pretoria during the Boer War.

However, these tragic events would not impact upon Daisy's life in any way as they would not occur until well after Morant's short-lived marriage to Daisy had failed, which it did after he was allegedly involved with some petty theft involving livestock around the station, similar to dealings he may have undertaken to pay for their wedding!

Daisy's reaction was swift and ruthless, immediately severing ties with Morant.

And yet, although she may have physically and emotionally divorced him, no official divorce papers were ever filed.

Thus, they remained married, at least in the eyes of the law.

Heading south, Daisy took up yet another governess position in Berry in NSW, meeting a cattleman and breaker of wild horses, Jack Bates. A brief courtship concluded in them marrying at Nowra in 1885.

Jack's profession was inherently nomadic, so not long after their marriage he had to resume droving, a profession not overly conducive to newly-wed happiness, especially for Daisy who had no desire to traipse all over the country living it rough and never having a 'proper house' to live in.

No sooner had Jack departed than Daisy moved almost immediately to Sydney where it is believed she married again, this time to Ernest Baghole, just four months after her union to Bates, something she kept secret from Baghole.

Baghole was the son of a wealthy London family, and Daisy had met her latest husband on-board *The Almora* only a few years before. This moment of polygamy was to be yet another short-lived affair as within months Daisy and Jack were reunited.

A year later, in what might be construed as her committing finally to a more conventional notion of married life, Daisy gave birth to a son, Albert Hamilton Bates, in Bathurst in August 1886.

Yet even this stab at motherhood did little to alter Daisy's more natural, boisterous and adventurous nature.

This is not to condemn or moralise about her character.

In all probability, Albert's birth may have been her hope that Jack would settle down so that they could finally be a 'normal' family.

Such was not to be the case.

Daisy found herself alone with Albert for long stretches, effectively husbandless (and yet in legal 'possession' of three husbands) as Jack pursued his career as a drover, leaving her unhappy.

And who, it must be asked, wouldn't be unhappy with this kind of relationship, never knowing when one might next see one's partner?

How could such a marriage survive?

Bates 'suffered' this life for several years, but eventually could no longer contain an attack of the wanderer's itch as it struck again with full force in 1894.

Detaching herself from both husband and young child, with little fanfare or explanation about what she would do, where she would go or when she would return, Daisy boarded *The Macquarie*, bound for England.

Her parting words to Jack were that she would only return when he could guarantee her an established, stable home.

What she might have said to the young Albert, one can only surmise, but this seeming abandonment of the boy must have acted as a lethal blow to the long-term health of their relationship, and is an interesting insight into how determined Daisy was to live a life of her choosing, even at the expense of this intimate maternal relationship.

Arriving penniless in England, the resilient and ever-resourceful Daisy was not long unemployed. Her sharp survival instinct and enquiring mind helped land her a job as a journalist at a new publication, *The Review of Reviews*.

The Review had recently been established by career journalist W.T.Stead, renowned as a great reformist in the final decades of the century, and certainly a man and employer with very liberal leanings, infused with a feminist bent, being the first London editor to pay men and women equally.

For five years Daisy cut her teeth as a journalist, immersed in the intellectual stimulation of working at a progressive and highly successful publication. During this period she was lucky to encounter many celebrities of the day, including such men as Sir Cecil Rhodes and George Bernard Shaw.

While this must have been more the life Daisy had hoped to live, in 1899, she was finally prompted to return to Australia.

Jack had contacted her with news suggesting he was looking to settle down, having his eyes on a property in Western Australia. This contact with her, seemingly within the conditions she had specified as being imperative for her return, coincided with allegations in *The Times* of certain atrocities occurring in North-western Australia against indigenous people.

It appeared fate was conspiring to see her return to Australia.

The journalist in her couldn't resist the call of such a story, and enough semblance of feelings for Jack remained such that his promises held an additional allure.

Taking passage aboard *The Stuttgart* for Perth, during the long journey she met Father Dean Martelli, a Catholic priest, who, like herself, was after an absence returning to Australia. He told her of his work with indigenous peoples, offering much useful insight into the kind of issues that faced them with the coming of white man and the inevitable clash that was occurring between the two vastly different cultures.

This additional knowledge must have further stoked the journalistic fires already burning in her to investigate *The Times* report that had initially stirred her to consider the return down-under.

On her arrival in Perth, Jack met her at the ship and almost immediately Daisy realised nothing much had changed. His promise of the mystery property purchase was still nothing more than that—a promise—and he had made little else of himself, having even physically deteriorated in her eye.

Little of the man she had fallen in love with fifteen years ago remained.

Even the sight of an unkempt Albert, who for years had lacked the love and support of a mother, seemed to stir little in the way of compassion or care in Daisy, except insofar as to having her see to his proper housing and placement in a school.

After some time bedding herself down in the small newspaper community of Perth, with Jack and Albert in tow she went to the Trappist mission at Beagle Bay, north of Broome, in search of the story she had come back to Australia to cover.

This was to be a life-changing experience for Daisy, both as a woman and journalist, as she was suddenly faced with some of the atrocities she had read of while in England. Not only were the local indigenous population being forced to work in slave-like conditions, they were also suffering many of the abuses reported in *The Times*—if not those of a more heinous nature.

To add to this dire situation, they were often also shown utter disregard as human beings in death. More than once Bates would see the still-chained bodies of the dead who had tried to flee their imprisonment but had been stalked and shot in their tracks for supposed 'disobedience'.

This did not sit well with Daisy on any level, and although she was not sure what she could do about it, at the very least it ignited in her a desire to begin documenting not only this but more generally the lives of indigenous peoples she came across.

It would be a watershed moment in her life and career.

In the meantime, Jack, true at long last to his word, secured some pastoral leases in the Murchison district. Daisy, however, returned with Albert to Perth, where she struggled to get by on some freelance journalist work.

The year 1902 saw her take up with Jack once more, this time on a droving trip from Broome to Perth, although it is likely Daisy saw this as much an opportunity to further her investigations as to be with her husband. These travels enabled her to forge connections with local tribes of the Broome district, noting and recording everything from their vocabularies to their many sacred rites and observations.

Thus, where this could conceivably have been a trip of reconciliation for Daisy, her son and husband, it instead acted as the main springboard for what would become her lifelong work.

Despite having no formal anthropological training, her first formalised study of indigenous peoples began in 1904 when she was commissioned by the WA government to investigate and research tribes throughout the state. This was later narrowed to a more confined study of the Bibbulmun tribe located in the south-west, allowing Daisy to devote herself to a concentrated study rather than the more far-reaching commission she had originally been offered.

For the next five years, essentially living among the Bibbulmun, Daisy watched and noted everything she could about the tribe. She recorded their social structures; their myths and religious beliefs; their language, with the aim of constructing a dictionary; inter-tribe relationships; and anything else she deemed noteworthy.

This information was continuously fed back to the government in the form of articles, reports and lectures. In recognition of her ongoing efforts, Daisy was made a fellow of the Royal Anthropological Institute of Great Britain and Ireland in 1907.

Throughout this period Daisy also continued her journalism, writing articles for various newspapers and magazines, not just on her own specific areas of interest but also on broader issues such as the growth being experienced in Western Australia as the state began its march towards becoming renowned as a mineral-rich frontier.

Papers more particular to her studies, such as *The diseases of native women* or *the Southern dialects and their relation to the Dravidian language* were snapped up by overseas publications and organisations, providing Daisy with more income to continue a body of work that, although still supported by the WA government, was now also becoming a passionate personal mission.

By 1910, she had gathered a substantial amount of information to allow her to put together a profoundly detailed manuscript as part of her commission. Daisy was, however, temporarily interrupted from completing her report when assigned to a British anthropological expedition led by A R Radcliffe-Browne and headed for the north-west of remote Western Australia.

This came at a time she was becoming more concerned with general welfare issues surrounding indigenous peoples, and began recalibrating her work along these lines.

Travelling with Radcliffe-Browne's party, Daisy's particular studies as part of the expedition were geared towards the health and hospitalisation of exiled natives of the islands of Bernier, many of whom she noted exhibited not just physical distress at their unsavoury situation, but also a great degree of mental anguish also. It was to be these men and women who, thankful for the tenderness and humanity with which she dealt with them, first offered her the affectionate title of 'Kabbarli'.

The expedition winding to a close coincided with the passing away of Jack, and ironically, after all his years of promises, he finally came good in death, leaving her a large cattle station and thousands of head of livestock. Seeing this as an opportunity to self-fund her 'work', she disposed of both station and livestock, which provided her with sufficient capital in 1912 to set up camp at Eucla among the Mirning tribe, or what was left of them, on the edge of the Nullarbor.

This became the first of several such isolated areas in which she would spend much of the rest of her life. During the eighteen months she spent there in her official capacity at Eucla as an 'Honorary Protector of Aborigines', Daisy began a true transformation. No longer was she merely a journalist and semi-professional ethnologist and anthropologist...she now began to see her role as much as a friend as anything else to the folk she lived amongst.

Drawn away briefly in 1914 by requests for her to attend meetings in Melbourne, Adelaide and Sydney where several interested parties were enthusiastic to discuss her findings and ongoing studies, upon completing her round of appointments she returned to reside with the Mirning people.

Daisy established a camp near Yalata where she would reside for several years until her resources began to run low. Wishing to continue her work uninterrupted by an impending dearth of finances, Daisy approached the South Australian government in the hope of attracting some funding, but was politely rebuffed.

Frustrated by this rejection, but not deterred, she moved to Ooldea, 800km from Port Augusta. It would be here at the site of a waterhole established during the construction of the Trans-Australian railway that she would spend the next sixteen years of her life.

Up until this point, and for the extensive period she would end up residing at Ooldea, she had no contact with Albert, and yet clearly still occasionally feeling some deep-seated maternal concern at where he might be, she tried to make contact with him towards the end of WWI. Learning he was serving in France, despite several attempts she was unable to establish a connection to him and subsequently ceased her efforts.

Her tireless work amongst indigenous peoples would eventually attract small grants of money and a sporadic stipend, although these were often meagre and not enough to realistically support her as she continued her life's great work. She also, when possible, continued to practice journalism, having articles published in various newspapers, periodicals and journals.

Despite the lack of financial support, those in power obviously considered what she was dong to be of value. Several times Daisy was called upon to present her ongoing findings to different government bodies, which it is argued resulted in the beginnings of government bedding down the notion of 'Public Health' specifically geared towards indigenous people.

Adding even more gravity and sense of import to Daisy's work were the numerous visits over the year she received from royalty and high-ranking officials, leading to the ultimate recognition of her work on 1 January 1931 when she was appointed a Commander of the Order of the British Empire (CBE) for her welfare work with indigenous peoples.

Not long after this tremendous public commendation, Ernestine Hill befriended Daisy.

Hill had forged a career for herself in the world of journalism, sitting alongside the man who would build an empire, Robert Clyde Packer, founder of the Packer media dynasty. Daisy's life and work yelled as a big story to Hill and so she gained approval to begin a syndicated series about her, *My Natives and I*, first published in *The Adelaide Advertiser* in 1936.

During this time, the money flowing to Daisy from the writing of the series enabled her to return to live in Adelaide, living in some small comfort after so many years in self-imposed hardship. Also in receipt of a small stipend from the government being paid to her to assist in the sorting of her reams of notes, with the further aim of compiling them into a comprehensive manuscript, she remained in Adelaide in the hope of completing this large and unwieldy project.

It was during this time that she would have a paper published, *The Passing of the Aborigines*, containing certain 'delicate' issues, including descriptions of the practice of cannibalism among certain tribes and her own personal provocative thoughts and ideas about the long-term prospects of indigenous people in Australia in the wake of the coming of white man.

This was not to be an isolated incident where Daisy would write, and have published, confrontational ideas…ideas so provocative, in fact, that they would cause something of an uproar at the time, miring her work in controversy.

Ideas that to this day still in some ways somewhat compromise her work.

In over 270 articles she wrote on indigenous life, cannibalism was mentioned and discussed several times. If this was not inflammatory enough, at least in the eyes of conservative white men who invariably took it out of context, Daisy also posited the assertion that it was imperative for no interbreeding to occur between indigenous Australians and white man. Her assumption was that any such interbreeding would be disastrous, leading eventually to the complete die-off of Australia's indigenous race, something that turned out to be completely incorrect.

Of course there is the possibility that Daisy was being more metaphorical in her declarations, as, given the somewhat parlous living state of different groups of indigenous peoples today, some might argue that the interbreeding of the two cultures, rather than 'actual physical' interbreeding of 'white and black' has potentially had a detrimental effect on indigenous lives and wellbeing.

But that's a discussion for a completely different book...

Despite the controversy over some of her more contentious conclusions, it cannot be doubted that her intentions were admirable, and that on balance she did far more good than harm with her work. Daisy's tireless efforts at trying to bring the welfare of the indigenous people she had lived amongst to the attention of government officials did pay off as policy makers at both State and Federal level began to realise they needed to formulate policy aimed squarely at indigenous people.

As if being called home, in 1941 she found her way back to the austere life she had lived for most of the twentieth century, shacking up in a railway siding in Wynbring, east of Ooldea, and attempting to continue her work, even as she reached the age of eighty and beyond.

By 1945, failing eyesight and general health issues forced Daisy back to Adelaide where she was housed in 'sanatorium', or what we would know today as an aged-care facility. After being placed in the sanatorium, even though decade upon decade had passed with no contact between mother and son, Daisy once more attempted to find Albert. These efforts were, however, to once again bear no fruit. The RSL was able to confirm he was alive, and living in New Zealand, but he refused to have any contact with her.

How this might have made her feel, we will ever know, although it would be reasonable to surmise that Daisy must have felt some disappointment at not being able to make some kind of peace with Albert.

On 17 October 1950, *the Adelaide Advertiser*[3] filed an article commemorating Daisy's 91st birthday celebrations, which, like much of her life, were kept on her own orders to an austere minimum. The article reported her to still be in lively spirits and able to walk relatively well, although her eyesight had diminished to such a point that she found it almost impossible to read.

Six months later, her long life, so much of which was dedicated to others (and yet, sadly, not to her own kin) ended on 18 April 1951. Daisy was buried, much as she would have preferred it, without undue ceremony at Adelaide's North Road Cemetery.

Some live their lives oblivious to the plights of those seemingly less fortunate than them.

Others are aware of the need to right wrongs, but feel powerless to do anything.

And then, in much smaller numbers, there are those individuals who decide to stand up for a cause, expending all their energy in their desire to ensure that what they believe as 'right' prevails.

Even taking into account some of the more debatable aspects of her life and character, few would argue that Daisy May Bates is a member of this last rare breed and still deserving of the native title bestowed upon her by the ancestors of those she lived amongst a century ago.

She is 'Kabbarli'.

---

3 The Advertiser (Adelaide, SA: 1931-1954), Tuesday 17 October 1950, page 6 c/- Trove resource, NLA

Katherine (Katie) Langloh Parker

1865-1940

Weeweemul is a big spirit that flies in the air; he takes the bodies of dead people away and eats them. That is why the dead are so closely watched before burial.

K Langloh Parker, *the Euahlayi Tribe*, 1905

This snippet of folkloric insight is one of many produced as part of a body of work by a woman who dedicated much time observing, and then documenting, the ways of the indigenous population native to the area in which she resided in north-west New South Wales.

Observing the tribes of her locale, she would note many such observations into the different aspects of indigenous culture, in particular indigenous folklore, culture and spiritual beliefs. Reading back on these writings, one can see they are framed through the somewhat restrictive and dated prism that comes with being of the Victorian-Era.

Thus, the writings are at times overladen with what ostensibly seems a degree of prejudice, containing a range of misconceptions.

Yet even taking such into account, the inherent value of such work in attempting to open up an understanding of indigenous culture must not be devalued, and thus it remains both intriguing and invaluable to this day.

CATHERINE ELIZA SOMERVILLE FIELD, or Katie as she would later prefer to be called, was born at *Luilyl*, her grandfather's property at Encounter Bay in South Australia, on 1 May 1865.

One of eight children born to Sophia Field and pastoralist husband Henry Field, Katie spent her early life growing up in Northern New South Wales after her father took up a sheep run on the Darling, establishing it as 'Marra Station'.

Given the fairly harmonious relationship that existed with some of the local native tribes, facilitated by regular employment of local indigenous men and women as stockmen, shepherds and domestic staff on her father's station, the young Katie was allowed to freely fraternise and form friendships with the indigenous children.

Little did Katie or her family know how fortuitous this connection would be—so fortuitous that it would ultimately result in the preservation of Katie's life.

One warm summer's day in January 1862, Katie and two of her sisters were taken by one of the domestic help, a young indigenous girl named Miola, to the Darling River to bathe. What should have been an innocent, fun-filled experience turned to calamity when the younger girls, one of them Katie, paddled out too far into the water and found themselves in trouble.

The elder sister, Jane, jumped into action in an attempt to avert a tragedy and save them, as did Miola, but the river was determined to take a life that day...or two.

Even as Miola managed to get Katie to the safety of the shore, Jane's valiant efforts were in vain as the river swept both her and four-year-old Henrietta away into its more treacherous currents where they drowned.

While clearly devastating to the Field family, they had no choice but to face the unpleasant fact that such a tragedy was part and parcel of the harsh reality of living in the outback.

So, they eventually recovered from the heart-wrenching loss— life simply had to go on.

As each child grew old enough to take on more serious responsibilities, Katie and her remaining siblings were given more constructive duties to perform around the property, from housework to caring for livestock to more general farm duties. They were home-schooled somewhat unconventionally by both parents, with Henry and his English classical education, so seemingly out of place in his working life on a sheep run, instructing them in ancient Greek culture and mythology.

Given Katie's own latter observations and writings, albeit focussed on indigenous peoples, Henry's passion for the classical clearly had a substantial impact on his daughter.

When her ageing mother fell surprisingly pregnant with her eighth child, in 1872 the Field family moved to Adelaide, wanting to be somewhere 'civilised' with appropriate facilities to accommodate the impending birth. The child was born in early April, and yet sadly, despite this move and the careful precautions to ensure an easy birth, such was not enough to ensure that the dangers that come with older women and childbirth could be avoided.

Just two weeks later, suffering 'childbed fever', Sophie died.

Unable to live in the house where his wife had so recently passed away, Henry moved the family to Glenelg where he took over the responsibility of running the household and caring for his children. Several years later, once he had found peace with his grief at the loss of his wife, he went on to re-marry.

Now in a 'city', albeit the small but growing capital of Adelaide, Katie was in a position to receive more formalised schooling, which she approached with relish. During this period she was introduced to Langloh Parker, a man sixteen years her senior.

This dashing figure had a reputation as something of a well-to-do socialite adventurer, but also had extensive hands-on experience as a cattleman, coming originally from a big cattle family. Parker's reputation and character were so well-known and highly regarded that he became the inspiration for a character in a story, *A Colonial Reformer*, written in 1876 by the prolific writer Rolf Boldrewood (the pseudonym used by Thomas Alexander Browne).

To the young, maybe slightly starry-eyed Katie, Langloh was an attractive option, as she was to him, so much so that they were married on 12 January 1875.

The years that followed were a whirlwind of social activity and travel for the newly betrothed girl, who found herself living a privileged and exciting life, moving in well-to-do social circles in Melbourne and Sydney.

However, this exciting new life finally looked like returning to something more approaching 'normal' when Langloh acquired a huge parcel of land on the Narran River, 'Bangate Station', near Angledool in far north New South Wales, just shy of the Queensland border, to which they promptly moved.

For the next five years Katie found herself immersed once more in the life of her childhood, albeit now in an adult role with all the duties and responsibilities that came with being a stationmaster's wife...except in one way.

Whether it was the readjustment back to a working life, and the burden of the obligations of such, or possibly her own mother's death in childbirth, or merely pure and simple personal choice by the couple, the Parker's remained childless.

One could surmise it was this 'gap' in her life, plus finding herself firmly settled into station life with a little more time on her hands, that helped fertilise a hunger for something more to do. Katie began observing and taking notes on the local indigenous tribes, in particular their vocabularies, with the hope of better understanding them. She focussed particularly on the Noongahburrahs, an indigenous people of the Narran River, who were a branch of the larger Euahlayi people.

As her grip on their language improved, although not professionally trained to collect their stories and folklore, she made a valiant attempt at recording as many of their oral traditions as she could.

Reports, however, do differ as to her actual relationship with the locals.

From her own personal amicable history with indigenous people, it would be easy to conclude that she forged friendly connections as she collected what would later go on to become her tales, with the locals happy to aid her in her exciting newfound 'work'.

And certainly, to be able to collect enough material to create two books would support the notion of a healthy and intimate association based on trust.

Contradicting this version of events, some reports indicate that, upon learning Katie had made public the very private information they shared with her, and not realising that this was her original intention when talking to them, certain members of the tribe were unhappy with their secrets being revealed.

Taken in this less-positive light, one could argue what Katie was engaging in was a form of cultural imperialism.

Whichever version of history one wishes to accept, Katie's written works were deemed more than suitable for publication. *Australian Legendary Tales* was published in 1896 as part of David Nutt's folklore series for children. It was followed up in 1898 by *More Australian Legendary Tales*.

Katie went on to receive some positive recognition and assessment of her work in 1897 when one publication, the *Australian Anthropological Journal*, praised her work, believing it to be meritorious and an important addition to literature on the indigenous peoples of Australia. However, despite this success and the effort Katie put in to create such meticulously written works, little academic commendation came her way, with neither book deemed of very much intellectual worth at the time.

This probably came as little surprise to Katie, or with much offense, as it would be fair to assume she was under no misapprehension while collecting the information that the tales would be destined for any kind of academic scrutiny.

A series of droughts and flooding so typical of the Australian outback, linked to the depression of the 1890s, meant that the highly-mortgaged 'Bangate Station' became no longer viable for the Parkers. In the late nineties they sold up and moved to Sydney, where just a few years later in 1903 Langloh died, aged sixty-two.

At just forty-seven, unencumbered by the responsibility of a property to manage or family to care for, Katie was clearly still young enough to consider a new life. Eighteen months after Langloh's death she set sail for England where she established residence and did some travelling through Europe. During this period she also finished writing up a dozen or so chapters from her diary, presenting them to a publisher.

These were appraised and considered commercially viable, printed the year after in 1906 under the title *The Euahlayi Tribe: A Study of Aboriginal life*. During this time she was also to meet the next great love of her life, Mr Percy Stow, whose father Randolph Stow, until his death in 1878, had been a prominent Australian politician.

A swift wooing and romance led to them being wed at a small ceremony at Westminster in November 1905. Not long after, they left England to return to Adelaide, Stow's home, which was also something of a homecoming for Katie given the time she had spent there decades before as a teen.

Returning home, taking back her original name and changing her surname to that of her new husband, 'Catherine Stow' slipped into a comfortable suburban life, so different to the outback existence she had known for periods of her life. Although far removed from those she had befriended, researched and observed when compiling the contents of her first books, Catherine still had notes and papers she hoped might be crafted into publishable material.

From these materials she went on to write two more books, both for children: *The Walkabouts of Wur-run-Nah* in 1918, and *Woggheeguy: Australian Aboriginal Legends* in 1930. Both had been loosely constructed years before, but not deemed suitable for addition in her earlier works.

Catherine was also actively engaged in her community, helping found the Victoria League of South Australia, of which she remained vice-president until 1939, and also setting up committees to help the Red Cross in their wartime activities during WWI.

In her mid-seventies, on 27 March 1940, she died peacefully.

At a time when women were more and more starting to make themselves known as intellectual equals of their male counter-parts, Katherine Langloh Parker added her own contribution to this in her endeavours to bring important aspects of indigenous culture to the attention of a wider world.

While some aspects of this may now read as politically incor-rect, it must be noted that they were, in terms of tone and lan-guage, very much 'of the time'.

Taking this into account, it would seem Parker genuinely believed in the great significance of the folklore and ways of the indigenous peoples she wrote of, wishing such to be preserved for the wider knowledge of humanity.

She was, at least for her time, a passionate collector of 'indig-enous legends'.

Jeannie Gunn

1870-1961

Full of bright hopes, we rested in that Land of Wait-a-while,
speaking of the years to come, when the bush-folk will have conquered the Never-Never...

Jeannie Gunn, *We of the Never Never*

Even today, the outback, and the way of life for those who brave it, is far removed from the comforts offered in the green, leafy suburbs of our major cities.

Adapting to such when moving from one to the other requires resilience, optimism and a willingness to embrace that which is 'other'.

So, imagine how much greater this challenge would be over 100 years ago when a young woman brought up in the suburb of Hawthorn in the growing city of Melbourne was whisked away by her husband to a cattle station over 400km from Darwin, just about as far away from home as possible…

…way out there in 'the Never Never'…

WHEN ONE COMPARES THE climate, flora and fauna, and geography of Scotland to that of Australia, it would be an understatement to say they are at the very least worlds apart.

And yet dire poverty, a range of epidemics and widespread famine in the nineteenth century generated enough disquiet, unhappiness and the search for a better life such that waves of Scottish immigrants began braving the long journey to the new colony.

As early as the 1820s, the newly-arrived Scots settled into the roles of farmers or livestock breeders in the largely uncharted wildernesses of the new country, or set themselves up as professionals in the growing settlements.

Further bolstered by immigration assistance schemes and the growing gold rush that seemed to be spreading across large swathes of the continent, the population of Scottish-born residents peaked at around 60,000 by the early 1860s, after this declining, but still remaining significant for some years to come.

In the midst of this massive influx came Thomas Johnstone Taylor and his wife Anne, heading to Melbourne at a time the city was rapidly expanding.

Ordained as a Baptist minister, just as his grandfather had been, (Thomas would later go on to set up his own business and also be on staff at *The Argus* for over twelve years), the couple committed to their new life and did what all young couples do—went forth and multiplied!

Their family grew rapidly so that by June 1870 the Taylor's produced their fifth, a girl they named Jeannie, who was born in the Melbourne suburb of Carlton, Victoria.

Jeannie was educated at home by her mother, as were all her siblings, and these studies were comprehensive enough that she would go on to matriculate at the University of Melbourne in 1887.

Just over a year after her matriculation, she and her two sisters established a private school in their own home in Hawthorn. They named it 'Rolyat' (Taylor, backwards) and slowly built up their student numbers until the school had a regular attendance of 50-60 pupils.

However, the marriage of one of Jeannie's sisters saw the school close down in 1896. Jeannie still retained the passion to teach and over the next five years took up different roles as a visiting teacher in various disciplines, including elocution and gymnastics.

During this period, her path would also cross with her future husband, Aeneas Gunn.

From Campbellfield in Victoria, and like Jeannie, the progeny of 'a man of the cloth', Aeneas had spent time as an adventurer in the top end of Australia, helping to establish a sheep station in the Kimberley's at the Princes Regent River. Aeneas would also offer assistance to Joseph Bradshaw as he attempted to set up his own run on the Victoria River before eventually feeling the pull to head back south to Melbourne.

Gunn embraced quite a different profession upon returning to his hometown, becoming librarian at the Prahran Library. He also took to writing of his experiences, having several of his stories published in 1899 as a series of articles in the *Prahran Telegraph*. These were of generally such a high quality that Gunn was eventually recognised professionally when elected as a Fellow of the Royal Geographic Society.

Around this time he met Jeannie, eight years his junior, whose diminutive form and spry manner immediately caught his attention. This romantic entanglement came at something of a watershed moment for Aeneas. Wanting once again to take up a life in the outback, he had just been appointed a manager at 'Elsey Cattle Station' on the Roper River.

This double stroke of good fortune drove Aeneas to his knees to propose to his newfound love and ask her to come with him on his adventure up north.

They married on New Year's Eve, 1901.

Soon after, the newlyweds were on their makeshift honeymoon aboard the steamship *Guthrie*, bound north for the port of Palmerston, the early incarnation of what would later become the city of Darwin. Arriving at the port, the first leg of their journey complete, following a brief respite they boarded the train for Pine Creek, and from there switched to horses, which they rode the rest of the way to the station.

For Jeannie, an educated schoolmistress who had rarely stepped afield from the gentile suburbs of Melbourne, this journey was understandably something of a shock to the system in being so far outside the realm of her life experiences so far. Once over this initial shock, however, she saw it as awe-inspiring in term of the landscapes she was traversing and the dawning realisation of just how much her life was about to change.

Jeannie initially had her detractors, men of course, both prior to her departure from Melbourne and also upon arriving at 'Elsey' who would argue that the station, and the outback more generally, was no place for a woman, especially a city-bred teacher like Jeannie.

How quickly she proved them wrong.

Those who met her were impressed by what they perceived as

an excellent sense of humour, fine horsemanship for someone still so new to riding and plucky nature at even attempting the journey to 'Elsey'.

Settling into life at the station, it did not take Jeannie long to fall in love with the land, about which she started keeping personal notes and musings that she would later go on to use in her writings. Like other women before her who were new to the outback and found themselves coming into contact with indigenous Australians for the first time, Jeannie began to reach out and form relationships with locals who either lived on the station as workers or drifted through. Offering them the warmth and friendship she would anyone, they began referring to her as 'good fellow missus' or 'the little missus'.

Unbeknownst to Jeannie, this new life she was happily embracing, and to which she was becoming somewhat attached, was soon to end abruptly as, to her great despair and ensuing loss, Aeneas contracted malarial dysentery, dying on 16 March 1903.

Given the connections she had forged with the locals, and more symbolically with the land itself, in the wake of Aeneas' death, Jeannie made the hard decision to return to Melbourne, no doubt torn to some degree about where her future lay.

Following just eighteen months on the land, Jeannie found the urban nature of Melbourne no longer to her liking, so took advantage of her father's travels and moved to Monbulk, a small settlement in the Dandenong Ranges, far from what she now perceived as the hustle and bustle of city life.

Here she resided in solitude, and over the next year received much encouragement from both friends and family, who had either read her letters while she had been up north or heard her telling stories to their children, to write about her time at 'Elsey'.

The Little Black Princess was the first complete work to come from the pen of Jeannie Gunn. Published in 1906 in both Australia and England, this children's book told the tale of Bett-Bett, based on an indigenous child at 'Elsey' Jeannie had known.

To this day still recognised as a realistic insight into indigenous culture and the attitude of turn-of-the-century white man to such, *The Little Black Princess* sold impressively for a first-time author and was well-received by critics, much to Jeannie's surprise and delight.

An inspired Gunn plumbed the creative well deeper following this success, and just two years later the novel she would become renowned for was complete.

We of the Never Never was published in 1908 and is revered as one of the early 'landscape' novels of its time for the degree to which it attempts to reconstruct precisely the region it is set in. Effectively a re-creation of actual events that occurred in Jeannie's own life during her time at 'Elsey', with just the names changed, it was sold as a novel and would go down in Australian literary history as a classic, even making its way into school curriculum.

By 1945, over 320,000 copies had been sold and it had been translated into German.

Sadly, Jeannie would not see any more of her work published for many years, and even then it would never have the impact of *We of the Never Never*.

This did not, however, mean she lay about idle, basking in her glory.

After a period of time travelling in Europe and undertaking some studies at the Sorbonne, she returned to Australia where, during WWI, she was very active in the area of 'soldier welfare' and that of their families, especially in her locale of Monbulk.

This would carry on post-war when she became a liaison for returned servicemen and the Repatriation Department, a role she would continue to hold in differing shapes and forms in the decades to come.

In 1939 she was awarded an OBE for both the dedicated welfare work she had engaged in over such an extended period, and also for her 'services to Australian Literature'.

Just four days after celebrating her 91st birthday, on 6 June 1961 Jeannie Gunn passed away, and, even taking into account the untimely death of her husband early in their marriage, while the bulk of her lifetime may have been spent 'travelling solo', she might be deemed as never truly being 'alone'.

Rather, her services to the community and the fact that she was constantly surrounded by both the superb stories she penned and the enjoyable characters within them, meant company was always nearby.

Years after Jeannie Gunn's death, *We of the Never Never* would have a second-coming of popularity when made into an Australian film, and would still often be named in lists of Australia's most popular books.

We of the Never Never would also be used later again in a unique way—one that Jeannie would never have envisaged and yet which meant it acted as a kind of legacy and payback to those she based some of its characters on.

In 1991 indigenous groups lodged a land claim through the Northern Land Council trying to establish who the traditional owners were in an area that happened to cover all of the old 'Elsey Station', something Gunn's book seemed to help support in their claim.

The result?

In February 2000, the traditional owners of 'Elsey Station' in the Top End of the Northern Territory were handed back full ownership of their country.

This wonderful, unexpected legacy of the novel is not to exonerate *We of the Never Never* from some criticism.

Not so dissimilar to certain condemnations levelled at the works of others writing about indigenous people at the time (K Langloh Parker, for example), contemporary analysts and academics have focussed on the allegedly racist elements of the work, or at least it's too European-centric attitude to its subjects, slanted to the condescending view of white man and his imperious opinions of indigenous peoples prior to their 'liberation'.

And yet, as with all such work, it must be viewed via the intention of its writer, which was to epitomise life as she saw it, with all the imputed values that came with the time in which it was written. To do otherwise would be deceitful, and to in any way edit Gunn's work as some show of political correctness would be an injustice not only to the writer but also to those it represented in terms of erasing or altering a past where indigenous people were too often viewed in a light that we see today as archaic, debasing and unfair.

Whichever way it is viewed, the work of Jeannie Gunn lives on to this day, and no doubt will continue to do so, from now...

...to *never never*...

Modern Amazons

20th-21st century

**_Don't wait for the light to appear at the end
of the tunnel, stride down there and light the
bloody thing yourself._**

Sara Henderson

Same same...but different...or really _bloody_ different at times!

This is how you might describe the lives of the women who
choose to live in the outback in contemporary Australia compared to that of those who came before them.

There may be more mod cons available to them than in the
past.

Given the improvement in modes of travel and with the advent
of better telecommunication, and in particular the Internet, they
may not suffer quite so much the tyranny of distance.

And certainly the nature of the manual work they must do in
their day-to-day lives may be somewhat easier due to advances
in technology.

Yet the outback itself is still what it has always been—one
moment awe-inspiring and wondrous, the next cruel and

unforgiving—filled with so many challenges that urban dwellers might never truly comprehend or be able to manage it.

And the women there are still doing their thing...being the outback amazons just as the women who came before them.

Mayse Young

1913-2006

Pubs hold their own special place in the Australian identity, a classic part of the Australian cultural and physical landscape, whether in the city or the outback.

In the latter, it could be argued, they play a particular importance in that they are so often the heart of many outback towns, especially those in the more remote regions of our immense country.

Their intrinsic value, however, far exceeds the vital status of them as a gathering place and watering hole for the locals or occasional passers-through. These establishments remain important centrepieces of towns from the Wye River in far-east of Victoria to Exmouth, way across the continent in the far-west. Pubs are places to congregate, catch up on town gossip, celebrate, and commiserate. They can be the general store or the post office, a counselling centre or a wedding function venue, the local 'Chinese' or the pizza parlour.

And standing behind every bar in every pub is the friendly publican: the man who keeps the whole thing running.

He'll pull you a beer, tell you a yarn, listen to your miseries or turf you out if you've had a few too many.

Or, 'she' will...

S O MANY NEW FRONTIERS expand quickly and then are consequentially strung together by the construction and continual expansion of their railroads, built via the back-breaking, sweat-inducing labour of the men who work them.

Mayse Dowling was born to such a man, railway ganger George Dowling, and his wife Evelyn in 1913 in northern Queensland.

Given his choice of occupation, for many years the Dowlings had no real concept of a stable 'home'. As each section of the line was laid, the work would move onwards, and thus the family was in almost constant motion, no sooner settling down at one camp than collecting their belongings together into their wagon for the horses to take them on their way to the next.

Life was rough and ready, and a ganger's wage wasn't the greatest, but George and Evelyn struggled as best they could to provide for their growing family. Times were generally lean and often only the bare essentials were available to them, sometimes not even these—for instance, Mayse didn't own a pair of shoes until she was nearly eleven!

The Dowlings lived in canvas tents and spent most of their time out of doors. The children only received the occasional session of schooling when near a town that had facilities, but were generally never settled in one place long enough to receive anything resembling a formal education.

In 1927, the railway work came to a halt at Mt Isa, leaving George at a loose-end work-wise. Not to be discouraged, he sold up the horse and cart and purchased an old Ford truck and Dodge car, loading them up with the family and their meagre possessions, and heading to the Northern Territory, following the stock route.

Here he found some ganging work, and so the Dowling's itinerant life continued, but only for a short time as once again the work dried up in 1929, with George left wondering what to do next.

As no new work options seemed likely, George decided that this presented the opportunity for a 'holiday', of sorts. So, over the next eight months the Dowlings journeyed down through Alice Springs to Port Augusta, an arduous expedition in those days consisting of unsealed roads and long stretches of nothing, but a wonderful opportunity for Mayse and her family to observe a part of the country they had never seen before.

Once in South Australia they crossed the Nullarbor Plain to Perth where George was hopeful of finding work. Unfortunately, nothing much was forthcoming, so the Dowlings continued onwards, weaving their way north to Broome then across the Kimberley's until they reached Katherine.

Setting up camp by the Katherine River, not quite knowing what to do next, out of the blue an opportunity arose for George to buy into the only pub at Pine Creek, which lay 90km north of Katherine.

At that time, Pine Creek was essentially a gold-mining town, although well past the heights of the rush that had brought up to 2000 Chinese to the area decades before. It was also an overnight stop on the train line to Darwin. Despite the tapering off of gold mining profitability in the area, the town remained alive and thriving, and was, if anything, slowly coming back into prominence as a mining town due to a growth in exploration leading to the discovery of other precious metals such as uranium, iron-ore, silver, lead and zinc.

With this new spurt of discovery came a swelling once more in the number of miners moving back to the area, and thus the town looked like remaining a hub for these workers.

So, into the pub the Dowling's moved, and unbeknownst to her at the time, this was to be the beginning of a lifelong association with and love of pubs for Mayse, and all that came with them.

More significantly at the time it was a home…a 'real' home.

Finally somewhere that actually had four walls and a roof.

A kitchen for her mother to cook meals in.

Beds to sleep in.

A bathroom.

No more campfires or being uprooted every time the work required it.

No more disruption.

Mayse quickly and happily adapted to the conclusion of her no-madic existence. Old enough to pitch in, she helped out around the pub, learning to make beds, clean, iron and wash, wait on tables and, once over the legal age, to perform the most important task of all—to pulls beers!

This provided a long overdue opportunity for the Dowlings to put down roots and be part of a community where they could make friends, improve the education of their children and generally have more of a conventional life.

For Mayse it also meant the arrival of love, and yet with it, ironically, a return to a life not dissimilar to that of her youth, at least for a few years.

In 1933 she married Joe Young, one of the many miners working the region. Given his profession and the need to live in close proximity to the mines, Mayse was once again back on the road and roughing it, camping in the bush in an iron hut and doing her best to provide a home for herself and her husband.

Falling pregnant in the shadow of the impending wet season, Mayse was shipped off to Melbourne to protect both her health and that of her unborn child, although she did return to Pine Creek after the birth.

This was, however, to be something of a short-lived homecoming as the advent of WWII brought a shadow of fear across the Top End of Australia.

With Japan a growingly active regional warring participant allied with Australia's enemies, a mass evacuation from the north of the continent commenced for fear of both air and sea attacks, forcing Mayse and her extended family from the area in 1941.

They sat out the war in safer climes, but when hostilities came to a close in 1945, the family were happy and relieved to be able to return to their beloved pub in Pine Creek.

Upon their return, joy turned quickly to despair when they found the pub extensively damaged (it had been used as rec. hall during the war) and their home destroyed.

Undetered, this proved to be but a minor inconvenience for the hardy Dowlings. Mayse and her extended clan restored the pub and rebuilt their homes—the heart of Pine Creek was pumping strongly once more!

This occurred just in time for a resurgence in mining as it began once more to gain prominence across the region.

Over the following decades, Mayse would mother seven children while continuing to be an industrious businesswoman, something still unusual for her day, especially in the outback. She would become known far and wide in her role as publican, going on to own several other pubs outside of Pine Creek. In the 1950s the family moved to Katherine where they bought into the Commercial Hotel and later would own a pub in Darwin, which, sadly, they would have to flee from in the approach of Cyclone Tracey in 1975.

The family also invested in various parcels of pastoral land, ensuring their finances were not just tied up in one venture.

Eddie Ah Toy, whose family had set up the local grocery store in Pine Creek in the 1930s, and who was just as much of piece of the landscape as the Dowling family and consequently the Young's, claimed Mayse to be the best looking publican in the country, and the most personable.

His is just one of many such glowing praises of her role as a publican—others spoke of her generosity, her good-natured attitude when faced with all manner of 'situations' and of her gentle nature.

These high praises were a product of Mayse's simple philosophy about running her business—no matter who came into her pubs, she treated every customer with respect, and thus felt she would always be accorded the same.

On the surface this might appear a fairly uncomplicated business formula, but given her success over many decades in different establishments it was clearly one that stood her in good stead during her many years of trading. The way she managed people is particularly admirable when one considers that Mayse must have dealt with every kind of patron imaginable: cattlemen, long isolated from civilisation taking a well-deserved drinking break from a muster; miners, with little else to spend their pay on but beers to slake their heavy thirsts after long periods of work down the mines; and always that vast assortment of tourists and itinerants passing through from every possible place and walk of life.

As if her long days of work and bringing up seven children were not enough, Mayse was also an active participant in most of the communities within which she resided. She volunteered for many different organisations and was even the first female elected as the President of the Pine Creek Race Club.

Mayse's lifelong work was formally recognised in 1994 when she received an Order of Australia for her work with the community. She would live on for almost another decade after this until, surrounded by her massive family of children, grand-children and great grandchildren, she died from pneumonia at the age of ninety-two in March 2006.

When over 200 people pack into a church (The Christ Church Cathedral in Darwin, no less) for a funeral, one can surmise the person's life being celebrated, and thus the person themself, must be far from ordinary. And when the funeral is for someone the likes of Mayse Young, few in attendance would argue she was the most 'extraordinary-ordinary' person they knew.

With her passing, Australia lost one of its great outback publicans, and great outback women—someone who will long be remembered for her solid business head, affable nature and open-minded absence of judgement towards the assortment of characters with whom she came into contact during her long, colourful life.

Faith Bandler

1918-

Fighting 'the good fight' for what we believe in and having our voice heard is the right of each and every individual—is the basis of the democratic tradition.

For some it starts off as a small trickle of discontent that grows in size and import until it is a torrent that sweeps their lives in one direction.

Others are thrust into it purely due to circumstance, but take up the challenge nonetheless.

And for others again, it is all they have ever known as the fight is fundamentally about who they are.

It is as close to them as the colour of their skin—a fight for their very existence.

And most often at the core of their struggle is a solid 'faith' in their beliefs, and holding true to that faith no matter the obstacles thrown their way.

THE FORCED RECRUITMENT OF labourers through trickery or undisguised kidnapping is referred to as 'Blackbirding'. In terms of the Australian experience, 'black-birded' souls were often sourced from the indigenous populations of the Pacific islands or northern Queensland.

In the 1860s and 70s, in a situation not unlike that of African slaves in the sixteenth and seventeenth centuries who were spirited away to the West Indies, Peru and later North America as indentured workers, such illicit human trafficking focused on supplying labourers to Australian plantations, particularly to Queensland sugarcane growers.

This trade was so great that over a period of thirty years it is estimated that up to 30,000 men and women were caught in this illicit and degrading indenture.

Peter Mussing was one of them.

A native of an island in the Vanuatu chain, he was taken in 1883, at around the age of thirteen, and transported to Mackay in Queensland. Not long after, he found himself working for his life on a sugar cane plantation.

This harrowing existence, so far away from his loved ones and home, would continue for fourteen years.

Desperate to break free from this servitude, Peter hatched an escape plan and successfully implemented it, immediately heading south to a new life. Free and finally able to make something of himself, Mussing met the person who would become his wife—a woman of Scottish-Indian heritage named Ida.

Following their marriage, they established a banana share-farm near Murwillumbah at Tumbulgum on the Tweed River in New South Wales, and it was here they would raise their children, and where their sixth child, Ida Faith Mussing, would be born on 27 September 1918.

Faith's early childhood would be spent predominantly helping out with the production and harvesting of fruit and vegetables her family grew on the farm. She has fond memories of her father, a devout Christian, playing records of American slave songs loud enough for them to be able to hear such as they went about their duties. He also at times preached in their local church, no doubt ever-thankful that his 'Saviour' had helped him escape the slave conditions under which he had once lived.

Peter's faith and prayers, however, would not be enough to save him from falling prey to the consequences of the rigours his body were forced to endure during the forced labour at the plantations for so many years.

In 1924, his life was tragically cut short when Faith was just five years old.

On his deathbed it is reported Peter remained positive, wanting to leave some final words of wisdom with Faith, telling her, 'Always look after this one', something the young girl might not have understood at the time but that unconsciously resonated with her for the rest of her days…the last words from a man who wanted his child never to bow to or be oppressed by others as he had for too-large a chunk of his prematurely-terminated life.

Following Peter's death, the family moved into the town of Murwillumbah where Faith began her education. What should have been a normal childhood experience for her sadly was not. Being an indigenous girl at a predominantly white school, she was emotionally abused and treated with an unfair degree of contempt.

And yet true to the maxim, 'What does not kill us makes us stronger', it would be this dose of 'bad education', linked to her father's appalling blackbirding ordeal, that would shape Faith's beliefs, sharpening her desire to see justice and equality for indigenous peoples later in life as an adult activist.

Like any family in a one-parent situation, life was tough.

Ida, a nurse, was bringing in some income, and Faith's older siblings—including her brother and mentor, William—did what they could to support the household, but it still often meant going without and making do wherever possible. Despite these hardships, Faith sat for her Higher School Certificate in 1932, the only non-white student to do so, and not long after left school to complete a dressmaker's apprenticeship in the big smoke, Sydney.

As WWII raged in Europe and Australians were called to arms, Faith and her sister Kath joined the cause, getting involved with the Australian Women's Land Army. Working on farms to grow various kinds of produce to feed the troops, Faith and, no doubt, many other women, experienced widespread sexism. This was also doled out with a heavy serving of racism as, while not an indigenous Australian herself, she was clearly a 'woman of colour', and, along with the indigenous women working around her, was paid less than other workers.

This period of employment would prove to be yet another paving stone on her road to activism.

With the end of the war in 1945, once discharged from her duties Faith moved back to Sydney. It was here, after a long affair with a Finnish sailor, that she would meet her lifetime partner, someone who had also experienced firsthand what it was to be marginalised and treated as 'lesser'.

Hans Bandler was a Jewish refugee from Austria. A mechanical engineer by trade, he had been picked up by the Nazi's in 1938 and imprisoned first in Dachau then Buchenwald before his aunt managed to secure his freedom.

Released in 1939, he fled to England, later aided in his passage to Australia by the help of some Australian doctor's he had met in Vienna. Embracing his new life, so much so that he soon became a citizen of his adopted country, one of his personal pleasures was music.

And it was while attending a musical evening put on by the Australia Peace Council that he came across Faith.

Several more outings to other musical events led to the pair officially 'dating', falling in love and going on to marry in 1952. They would have a daughter, Lilon, and also foster an indigenous boy, Peter, who they found abandoned in a park.

Their home became a meeting ground for all kinds of activity, often of a musical or artistic bent, and with this, as is often the case, came liberal thinkers interested in political change. Mingling with such progressive type was just what Faith needed to begin formalising her ideas about wanting to do something to foster change in the way indigenous Australians were viewed and treated by the community around them.

After a chance meeting with Pearl Gibbs, a well-known indigenous activist, the pair quickly became friend and colleagues, establishing the Aboriginal-Australian Fellowship in 1956 as the vehicle for their cause.

Over the next fifteen years, Faith would work with a range of men and women, all equally devoted to her mission, including radical activist Jessie Street, Jack and Jean Horner, Emil and Hannah Witton, and Ken Brindle, among others.

In 1963 she became the state secretary of the Federal Council for Aboriginal Advancement, which would later be expanded to become the Federal Council for the Advancement of Aborigines and Torres Straits Islands (FCAATSI) in 1967. At around the same time, the biggest challenge, that would later become her greatest triumph, was handed to Faith.

The Federal Government, after much lobbying by passionate political activists like Faith, had finally agreed to hold a referendum asking Australians to vote on whether the Constitution should be altered to ensure indigenous peoples had the same rights as other Australian citizens.

Faith was appointed the NSW campaign director, something she took up with energy and gusto as in so many ways it represented the answer to her life's work. From Faith's perspective this was a moment in history where things could change forever—where there would no longer be, at least in the pages of Australia's primary and most powerful legal document, the Constitution, a distinction between 'black' and 'white'.

Lobbying hard for a 'YES' in the referendum, Faith addressed hundreds of political meetings and rallies, using her charisma, media skills and natural speaking ability to change the views 'white' Australians had of indigenous peoples.

After months of such work, the time for Australians to vote came.

And to the exultation of Faith and all those who had strived with her to see this momentous change come about, her hard work and dedication paid off—the referendum was passed with 90.2 per cent of the vote.

Despite the initial jubilation at the passing of the referendum, Faith's work was by no means over. This enshrinement of equality in the bedrock of Australia's legislative and judicial system, while clearly a major hurdle to cross in addressing racism, was still just the beginning of addressing 'actual' racism and inequality at a day-to-day level across the country.

For the next five years Faith continued her politically-active life, going on to co-found the Women's Electoral Lobby in 1972 and the National Commission for Australian South Sea Islanders in 1974.

Having done so much in her twenty-odd years as an activist, it was around this time that she felt it was time to resign from political life, while still remaining a strident voice for the further advancement of indigenous rights.

Retired, and with some much welcomed time on her hands, Faith visited for the first time the island of Ambrym where her father was born. This journey struck within her a powerful desire to tell her father's story, and also to expose the blackbirding of the previous century for what it was—slavery.

His tale she went on to tell in a book *Wacvie* (his native name), published in 1977. This was to be one of many books Faith would write or co-write. Others included *Mariani in Australia* (with Len Fox 1980); *Welou, My Brother* (1984); *The Time was Ripe* (with Len Fox); and *Turning the Tide* (1989), the latter two being personal accounts of the Aboriginal-Australian Fellowship and FCAATSI respectively.

As recognition of her tireless efforts in trying to secure the welfare of indigenous Australians, Faith was appointed a Member of the Order of Australia (OAM) in June 1984 and was named one of Australia's '100 Living Treasures' by the National Trust. In January 2009, she was appointed a Companion of the Order of Australia (AC), adding yet another illustrious title to her revered name, although sadly in September of that same year, after 57 years of marriage, Hans was to pass away.

While not one of our more typical outback Amazons, having been brought up in the outback and given the great good she has done for so many indigenous women, it is fitting for Faith Bandler to be included in this collection.

At the age of 92, Faith is alive and well, a woman worthy of national treasure status, and a part of the essential bedrock of a 'better' Australia.

And while there still remains what might appear a rocky road to be travelled in improving more the lives of indigenous peoples, Faith's tireless work will always be remembered as an historical turning point in at least the right direction towards an Australia where colour is not the defining factor of a man or woman's destiny, but rather merely the skin they were born in.

Molly Clark

1924-

The word 'Andado' is derived from the southern Aranda term for a 'stone implement.'

Thus, it would come as no surprise that the station of the same name is located way out 'back of burke', just about as isolated as a place could be…and to survive a long life so far removed from a conventional existence, any man—or woman—would have to have a will carved from stone.

In fact, they would need a resolve so stony that nothing seems an obstacle: not the heat; not the isolation; and certainly not the flies, the hundreds and thousands of which thrive the whole year round, come rain or shine.

Even the untimely death of the man who has been by your side for forty years, although a life-changing event, would have to be absorbed like granite.

Such a person would need a heart as solid and enduring as a rock: that could stand firm against despair and loss and loneliness, because above all else, their love of the land surpasses all.

ABOUT 350KMS AS THE crow flies from Alice Springs, lies 'Old Andado Station'. It sits fifteen kilometres inside the Simpson Desert, which, with an area of 176,500 km², is the fourth largest in Australia.

In 1880, Willoby and Gordon first held part of the land 'Andado' would later be established on, although it was not until nearly thirty years later that Robert Sharpe and David Mayfield would formally occupy it.

As WWI blazed in Europe, George McDill acquired grazing land in the region and in the early 1920s built a more formal homestead: following some good rains, he and partners Robert McDill and Henry Roper introduced sheep to the station.

Typical of the uncertainty of the climate in the outback, an extensive drought followed not long after, and yet despite the potential for ruin, the McDills hung on so that by 1933 they were running a property with 1300 sheep and 420 cattle.

The property went on to change hands several times over the next decade or two until May 1955 when owner H.H. Overton formed a partnership, 'The Andado Pastoral Company,' with one of his overseers: Malcolm 'Mac' Clark and wife Molly.

Molly was a South Australian, born in 1924 in Mount Barker. Initially she pursued a career in nursing, moving at the age of eighteen to Adelaide, but gave up her profession after suffering a bout of Tuberculosis, possibly contracted while undertaking her duties.

Mac and Molly met in the 1940's when the latter held a position as a governess at 'Mungeranie Station' on the Birdsville track. They struck up a friendship that progressed to a relationship, the pair going on to marry in 1946.

After Mac was employed as an overseer in 1949 by Overton, the couple must have seen some great potential in working this large station, reflected in their choice just over five years later of taking up the offer of a partnership with Overton when it was made to them.

In 1955, with three sons to care for, Mac and Molly commenced a true labour of love, pouring blood and sweat (and much later, unbeknownst to Molly at the time, tears) into making something of 'Andado'. They refused to be beaten by unpredictable elements that could bring flooding rains one season and drought the next. Even when the heavy rains made the original homestead unliveable one year, they would not be forced from the land, instead building a new dwelling eighteen kilometres west of the old.

So far removed from civilisation, life on 'Andado' was never easy. Without even what some would consider bare essentials, such as electricity and hot water, Molly had to rely on the basics: kerosene lamps, candles, lanterns and a wooden stove. She just made do with what she had, an effort that did not go unrewarded when in 1969 the Clarks became the proud owners of the property, taking control of it outright.

All the years of hardship and sacrifice were paid off in full!

A few years later, ever the enterprising woman, Molly set out to restore the ruined older homestead to its former glory. Having a desire to show tourists how life was back in the early days, with the help of her family she established the Tjauritchi Wanda Tours business.

Life seemed as good as it could be, but unfortunately, the subsequent years would contain multiple tragedies for the Clarks, particularly Molly.

In 1975, a near-miss occurred when her son Kevin was involved in a major car accident, but survived, much to the family's relief.

This was, however, the precursor to much greater misfortune that would rip the guts out of Molly's life.

Just three years later, while flying his light aircraft, Mac suffered a heart attack and died.

If this wasn't enough grief for a loving wife to bear, not long after this great loss, Molly's eldest son Graham was killed when his semi-trailer collided with a freight train.

This double-barrelled tragedy would be enough to lay low most 'normal' folk, but Molly was made of tougher stuff. Knowing that someone had to continue the legacy of the decades of hard work they had put into 'Andado', she pushed through the pain and continued to run the business.

So, life went on for Molly and 'Andado', albeit in the absence of two of her most precious loved ones...that is until the third and final chapter of Molly's misfortune presented itself—an event that would hit at the very heart of her livelihood and almost force her from the land she loved.

In the 1980s 'Andado' became one of the first cattle stations in the Northern Territory to undergo Brucelosis and Tuberculosis testing. Regrettably for Molly, with the property sitting on the South Australia border, she was forced to cull her entire herd.

Every last single beast.

What station can exist without its livestock?

Certainly not 'Andado'.

Having been battered with such a litany of personal tragedy and woe, and with the property reduced to being financially worth near to zero, Molly was forced to sell it for next to nothing.

Yet even at this seeming low-point, Molly was not to be deterred, managing to secure a Crown Lease over forty-five square kilometres around the homestead, renaming it 'Old Andado'. She ran this new venture as a tourist attraction where visitors could camp, be cooked for personally by Molly and take tours of the old homestead.

Over time, the property began to gain national interest, with up to 1000 visitors per month. This was formally recognised in 1993 when Molly's home was listed in the Heritage Register, and then, on a more personal level, when she received a Brolga Award (the official tourism awards program for the Northern Territory) in 1995 for her achievements in tourism.

She also went on to receive the 1998 NT Chief Minister's Women's achievement award, and a year later, a Commonwealth Recognition Award for Senior Australians.

During this time, Molly began to realise that women of the outback who lived and worked alongside their men were under-represented in institutions such as the Stockman's Hall of Fame in Longreach.

Consequently, she established the National Pioneer Women's Hall of Fame in the old courthouse in Alice Springs. A more permanent site was eventually found, and in March 2007 the Hall of Fame was re-opened in the old jailhouse.

Just prior to the opening, after fifty years living at 'Andado', a combination of ill health and a concerned family saw Molly moved permanently to Alice Springs, where she still lives.

Even without Molly's physical presence, 'Old Andado' carries on, still infused with her spirit and determination.

Surviving on small donations from visitors and a once-yearly fundraising drive, aptly called 'Molly's Bash,' the property is managed by a series of caretakers.

Given Molly's deep connection to 'Andado', it is in all likelihood never far from the mind of the near-ninety-year-old, who lives on, still full of life, looking like she might just crack the tonne.

After the remarkable, hard-fought life she has lived, would anyone be that surprised, if she did?

Sara Henderson

1936-2005

As many will know from the trying experiences they have had at one time or another, adversity presents itself in so many forms.

In the outback, it often comes as the most obvious—the whims of nature, generally, such as droughts, floods and pestilence.

There is, too, the great tyranny of distance that is part and parcel with living in the outback, which can exacerbate feelings of isolation and loneliness, taking adversity to a more psychological level.

Add in, for good measure, more personal concerns like ailing health, infidelity and family squabbles, and life suddenly is complicated, possibly even overwhelming.

Some might burn out at this point.

Others might flee a life that seems more burden than pleasure.

And others again will stand tall against the predicaments that threaten to topple them, and face them head on, unfazed by the challenge.

Rather than be weakened or destroyed by such, they instead go 'from strength to strength...'

ARA HENDERSON, WAS A woman who seemed always able to stand up to any obstacle that might present itself to her, prevailing against adversity and trying to turn it to her favour.

Born on 15 Sept 1936 in Mosman, NSW, to a publican father and stay-at-home mother, Sara's early life was typical of many children at the time. She lived in the relative comfort of a suburban middle-class family, although the coming of WWII obviously affected her in the same way it did so many others.

Once the war had passed, life began to return to normal and Sara found herself happily engaged, like most of her girlfriends, at the age of nineteen.

This happiness, however, was to be shattered as she faced her first great life challenge.

Out for a joy ride with then fiancé Ben in a new car purchased for him by his parents, the young man decided to put the vehicle through its paces, with disastrous results...a terrible car accident.

Sara sustained major injuries, including five fractures, a crushed left hip and extensive damage to her left knee. This would result in her spending many months in rehabilitation, with doctors unsure as to how her recovery would go and questioning what physical issues might potentially plague her after such extensive injuries.

Even at this young age, Sara proved she was made of strong stuff. Doctors marvelled at how well her bones knitted together, her body fully recovering to the extent that she could once more take up one of her personal favourite past-times, tennis.

Her relationship with Ben, however, would not be so lucky in surviving the accident as it fizzled away to nothing during the recovery.

As life regained some sense of normality, the twenty-three-year old Sara felt things were on the up again. She had a new job she enjoyed and was back in the dating game, having recently met a farm equipment salesman, Neville, while travelling on business.

It was at this happy and seemingly stable point in her life that a man literally sailed in, and in his debonair way changed it forever.

While Sara lay sunbaking one day at Mosman marina, a dashing American, Charles English Henderson III, approached her. The meeting was brief, and somewhat clumsy, but it resonated in her and would turn out to be fateful for them both.

Following this first, brief, but clearly memorable, encounter, Charles was intent on pursuing Sara. Soon after, that very same night, he managed to stumble across her at dinner, 'stumble' being a loose term: so interested in Sara was he, that Charles had done some research to find out exactly where she would be to ensure their paths would cross once more!

This second encounter alerted them both to the fact that they shared some kind of connection beyond the ordinary.

Over the next few months he wooed her, and while often away for extended periods in Hong Kong taking care of his shipping business partnership, the relationship still managed to flourish via correspondence or during the short breaks he took back in Sydney. Love blossomed, something they openly admitted to one another on Charles' return to Sydney for a five-day break.

Overjoyed at their shared feelings for one another, the love bubble almost instantly burst when Charles dropped a bombshell—an admission that Sara had sensed for some time was coming, but the nature of which she could not guess.

He was married.

With children.

And, to top it off, they lived in Sydney!

All this, just as he was about to fly out.

A shattered Sara could not believe what she was hearing, and this might easily have been the end of their relationship had Charles not immediately followed his admission up on his next visit back to Sydney with the revelation that he was as close as six weeks away from being divorced.

Relieved, the relationship continued, and once legally able to, the couple married.

The first few years of married life were spent outside of Australia, primarily in the Philippines, where, in her own words, Sara felt like 'she had it all'.

Unfortunately for her, Charles liked to 'have it all' also…or at least have something more than his relationship with her.

Learning he had been unfaithful to such an extent that he had fathered a child by another woman was crushing, and yet Sara stood strong, remaining with him for the sake of her own new family.

Following this potentially relationship-ending discovery, the Henderson's returned to Australia. The shipping business having gone under, Charles decided to make a go of running cattle, and had, accordingly, acquired a station of some 500 000 acres over 800km south-west of Darwin.

'Bullo River Station'.

This new venture would prove to be a radical change of life and circumstance for the city-bred Sara. Arriving at the property, it became instantly apparent that it lacked the most basic facilities, and she found herself living an almost Spartan-like existence.

Yet, as she had proven several times in different ways in her life so far, she was a survivor, and so survive she did, bringing up her family while working long, hard hours alongside Charles in his efforts to build the station up into a profitable business.

By the mid-sixties, they had put in enough time and effort to see things running smoothly enough for Charles to feel comfortable leaving 'Bullo' in the hands of his manager, and to take something of a 'sabbatical'. Having not seen his mother in many years, he proposed they take an extended trip to visit her in Maryland, USA.

This trip extended to a five-year visit.

While in the USA, infidelity would sadly become an issue again and their relationship would be compromised, although both refused to walk away from it. Ironically countering this was an extreme possessiveness and jealousy on Charles behalf. He could see other men were attracted to Sara and would not have it, regardless of his own wandering eye and indiscretions.

Their time in Charles' home country came to an end in 1971 when a return to Australia became imperative to try and rescue their cattle business, which had begun to founder. With the price of beef plummeting, back at 'Bullo' Charles and Sara and the rest of the family put their shoulders to the wheel, doing all in their power to keep the station a going concern.

It was touch-and-go for an extended period, and their debts grew to massive proportions, but slowly over nearly a decade the price of beef rose and it appeared their efforts would not be in vain. During this period Charles' health waxed and waned, but despite this failing of his body he would not be deterred from doing all in his power to see 'Bullo' stay afloat.

His marriage, though, was heading for less steady waters.

Following decades of being together, Sara and Charles officially separated in 1983. And yet with his health in serious decline, Sara stuck by the man she had spent her entire adult life with, offering whatever support she could until his body finally gave in and he died in June 1986.

The timing could not have been worse for Sara, whose elderly mother also suffered a stroke at around the same time.

Yet again, Sara was up to the challenge and did not falter.

Carrying the burden of her ill mother, a recently-deceased ex-husband and the crippling debt 'Bullo' still had hanging over it, accompanied by legal threats calling for payments owing, Sara carried on with the support of daughter Marlee.

At the edge of financial ruin, fate shone kindly at last upon Sara when some prudent stock investments came through at just the right time, saving her and her beloved 'Bullo'. And by her side, working tirelessly to try and keep the station going, was daughter Marlee.

So impressed was Marlee with her mother's strength that in 1990 she nominated Sara for 'Business Woman of the Year'. To both their surprises, but also their delight, Sara went on to win the award in 1991 in recognition of having turned around the huge debt the station carried and not losing it in the process.

From this came other opportunities, most importantly a book contract.

With such an interesting life-time behind her, and still before her, Sara began writing her autobiography.

From Strength to Strength was published in 1993 and became a best-selling autobiography. (Later, Marlee would contend that some of the book was really more 'memoir' than true autobiography because there were certain situations Sara wrote about that happened, but within which Sara was not necessarily an active participant.) The story captured the hearts of those who read it and propelled Sara into outback celebrity status. She went on to write several more books: *The Strength of Our Dreams*, *Some of My Friends Have Tails*, *Outback Wisdom* and *A Year at Bullo*.

As an eventful and successful decade wound to a close, Sara, in her early sixties, began feeling it was time for a slightly easier life...and the only way to allow for this was to sell 'Bullo'.

This decision, while completely understandable under the circumstances, would sadly mark an unhappy period for her and Marlee.

Having invested so much time and effort in 'Bullo' over the past fifteen years, Marlee felt she had some rightful claim over the property. Discussions over this with her mother broke down when it became clear Sara had a certain sum in mind in terms of the property's worth that clearly did not take into account Marlee's long years spent working there.

After rounds of offers and counter-offers, they were making no real headway and their relationship was souring to the point that settling the matter in court appeared the only option.

However, in an out of court settlement the 'situation' was eventually resolved. In March 2001 Sara sold 'Bullo' to Marlee and husband Franz, ending a bitter legal and personal family stoush.

It was also, regrettably, effectively the end of the once-close relationship between mother and daughter, who rarely spoke after the matter was settled.

In an ironic twist of fate, after having been the face of *Breast-*

Screen Australia for several years and appearing in a series of television commercials urging women in their fifties to have mammograms, Sara received bad news in 2002: she was diagnosed with a tumour in her right breast.

She went into surgery, with doctors immediately removing the cancerous growth. Given an excellent chance of living cancer-free, oncologists telling Sara there was only a five per cent chance of the cancer returning.

This time, however, luck was not to be on her side.

Sara would fall prey once again to cancer, in the form of leukaemia, and despite the strength she had exhibited for so much of her life, in late April 2005, after several months in hospital, at the age of sixty-eight she passed away.

Death being the great leveller, Marlee, set aside the bad blood that had come from the legal wrangling over 'Bullo' and out of respect attended Sara's funeral, with fifty or so others, at the Sunshine Coast's Caloundra St Andrews Anglican Church.

Clearly with the kind of woman Sara was, and knowing the life she had led, rector Bill Crossman took his reading for the funeral from St Paul's Second Letter to the Corinthians...

'Therefore we do not lose heart. Though outwardly we are wasting away, yet inwardly we are being renewed day by day...'

In the epilogue to *From Strength to Strength*, despite the patchy moments in their many years as a couple, Sara Henderson proudly acknowledges that she would not be the person she was, were it not for Charles English Henderson III.

While it is irrefutable that his presence in her life propelled her into a world filled with challenge after challenge in nearly every aspect of her life, something must be said for the kind of steely resolve she herself had to intrinsically have to take up that challenges and make the best of life she could.

Which is precisely, from all reports, what Sara did until her strength could sustain her no longer, and the time for true rest came…

Terry Underwood

1945-

Life is so often filled with chance encounters that bring with them unintended consequences.

We can be going about our daily lives and suddenly something occurs or we meet someone who will throw us onto a completely different path.

A path that leads us to a life we might never have expected.

A path filled with challenges and moments of wonder.

A path that takes us 'into the middle of nowhere'...

...to a place we actually would rather be than just about any-where else...

IF ONE COULD TRAVEL back in time to the Albury of the 1950s, arriving there one would find it to be as close to the idyll of what might be expected of a typical Australian country munici-pality of the era.

Albury had only gained official 'city' status in 1946, with a population of just 15,000, a far cry from the more than 100,000 who currently populate the now thriving border town that twins with Wodonga on the Victorian side of the great Murray River.

It was into this community that Terry Augustus was born in 1945, just prior to Albury's official 'town-ing', and where she would spend the first decade of her life, and she remembers her childhood fondly.

Books were important, and from an early age she took to writ-ing—poetry and short stories for the most. So proud was she of her work that she submitted pieces to *The Catholic Weekly*, which were duly published. She also recalls being quite sure at even such a young age that one day she would write a much longer work, her autobiography, although not until she had lived a long life as a farmer's wife first!

Relocating with her family in the late fifties to the booming post-war metropolis of Sydney, as she approached adulthood, Terry took up nursing—a fortuitous choice that would ultimate-ly, if not in the way she could have predicted at the time, deter-mine the shape of the rest of her life.

In 1963, the eighteen-year-old Terry, in the second year of her nursing training, received into intensive care at St Vincent's Hos-pital, in her own words, 'a strapping young stockman' from the Northern Territory.

John Underwood, three years her senior, had broken his back

when a horse rolled on him, had been operated on and received a spinal fusion, and thus was extensively plastered up and requiring comprehensive care, something Terry provided with due dedication.

Late at night as she worked on his pressure points, John would tell her of life in the remote outback, a life she found it hard to imagine, but was fascinated by. Whether it was this close and constant professional care she was required to give, or some more immediate and innate attraction (it's said John told his ward-mate at St Vincent's the first night he came into contact with Terry that he would marry her), a friendship developed that would mean this would be no brief encounter restricted to nurse and patient.

When John was released, he returned to the Territory, but not without a promise that he and Terry would retain some contact…contact initiated less than a week later when Terry received a postcard from him saying 'I think you're a bit of a darling, love John.'

This 'contact' became a courtship of several years via correspondence. John eventually invited Terry to his family property, about 600kms from Katherine, where Terry saw first-hand the life he lived, a life on some levels alienating in how different it was to the life she to which she was accustomed and yet fascinating.

Returning home, Terry and John continued their correspondence until John took the next step, flying to Sydney where he proposed.

Terry accepted, they were engaged and then married in Sydney, and suddenly that childhood dream of marrying her farmer had come true, albeit in a slightly different fashion to that which she had originally envisaged.

Nonetheless, the first part of 'the dream' had become reality.

Not long after, the newly married couple packed up Terry's worldly belongings and headed north to where John had secured a property he intended developing into a successful cattle station.

Having experienced a taste of life in the outback from their correspondence and her visit, upon arriving Terry had a fairly immediate sense of how dramatically her life was about to change. While many brides look forward to that day their new groom either literally, or metaphorically, carries them across the threshold of the new home, although there was certainly an 'abode' of sorts awaiting them at their new property, it was not quite the type maybe most brides would hope for.

On the banks of a dry creek-bed stood a bough shed that was to be their 'connubial dwelling' and from where they would begin this grand prospect of establishing John's cattle business.

So began the story of 'Riveren Station'.

The early days were a challenge.

Six hundred miles, literally in the middle of nowhere, without electricity or running water, made for rough living. Despite the heartbreak of losing her first child, Terry adapted quickly to both the terrible loss and the harsh life, doing so while raising a family (they would end up with four children: Marie, Patrick, Michael and Becky) and helping John run the business.

Being so remote meant the children's education had to be conducted through correspondence via Katherine School of the Air. This worthy organisation would catch Terry's broader interest, even after her children no longer required it, and she ended up holding positions on the Katherine School of the Air Associates and Council, and the Isolated Children and Parents' Association.

Holding these kinds of positions saw the commencement of a period during which Terry began building something of an outback profile for herself.

From 1984 she become involved with the Northern Territory Cattleman's Association and was an inaugural member of the Northern Territory Women's Advisory Council. In 1997 she became the first woman in forty-six years to open the Royal Darwin Show, and a year later was winner of the 'Business Owner' category of the Northern Territory Telstra Business Women's Owner Awards.

Busy as she was with her immersion in the business of helping run 'Riveren', and being involved with various important organisations, it was during this period that Terry decided a long overdue return to writing had finally come.

It was time to finally fulfil the second part of that childhood dream.

Terry began writing in the little time she had, sometimes up as late (or is it early?) as 3am, working through until 6am each morning, this being one of the only free and consecutive runs of hours she had available to her.

This painstaking literary labour, however, proved more than worth it, bearing a 'bouncing baby book', that would go on to be hailed as an inspiring tale: *In the Middle of Nowhere* was the end result of her renewed relationship with the written word.

Little did Terry know that she was writing a book that would be both well-received and that would eventually be labelled a modern Australian classic.

This autobiographical work, the core of which revolves around her enduring love and solid relationship with John, received its fair share of critical acclaim.

'The writing is splendid, and her description of the difficulties and tribulations of life in the outback ...paint such a clear picture of living problems presented by remote parts of Australia...'

Canberra Times

'It's a book in the genre of *We of the Never Never*, about a woman's growing love for her man and his country ... It's a book for Territorians to be proud of, an important addition to the story of how the Territory came to be what it is today.

Northern Territory News

'Terry Underwood is all the things a person SHOULD be... she's brave, gutsy, loyal, funny, smart and interesting. That's quite a tribute, but then Terry is quite a woman....*In the Middle of Nowhere* sounds like a good place to live.'

Wentworth Courier

'...one cannot dispute that it is a special woman's story of her family and the people who mean most to her. It is Terry's way of sharing her outback life experiences with others. She tells it simplistically with warmth and from the heart.'

The Age

With these favourable reviews, her book gained more attention as over 100,000 copies marched off the shelves. This wonderful outcome to her literary labours enhanced even further Terry's growing public profile.

In 2000, she was awarded life membership of the Northern Territory Cattleman's association, and a year later was named an ambassador for the *2002 Australian Year of the Outback*.

However, Terry's newfound celebrity status did not affect her commitment to the station and its cattle business, with which she continued to be actively involved.

The family went on to buy more stations in the Douglas Daly, almost 600kms north of 'Riveren'—the 'Midway Station' in 2004 and adjoining 'Inverway Station' in 2007. During this time, Terry was to be offered yet another acclamation in tribute to her commitment to the land, one, it might be said, she could surely never have imagined even in her most fantastical childhood dreams.

In 2005 Terry Underwood was named in the Queen's Birthday Honour list, awarded a Medal of the Order of Australia in the General Division and becoming 'Terry Underwood OAM'.

Near-on six decades of life had culminated in what many might consider one of the ultimate, national forms of recognition.

Now approaching her late-sixties, Terry Underwood OAM remains an active and modern role-model to women from far and wide, whether they live in the far reaches of the Australian outback or in one of our densely populated urban centres.

In 2012, a combination of factors prompted Terry and John to make the momentous decision to sell 'Riveren'.

Heading into retirement, they intend to move closer to their family, and yet after so many years on the land, part of Terry will no doubt remain firmly connected to the land she grew to love *in the middle of nowhere...*

Robyn Davidson

1950-

I've been through the desert on a horse with no name
It felt good to be out of the rain
In the desert you can remember your name
'Cause there ain't no one for to give you no pain...

(*America*, Dewey Bunnell 1971)

The classic 1970s ballad, *A Horse with no Name*, that propelled English-American folk band America into fame in the music charts might conceivably have had some deeper resonance for a young Australian woman who undertook her very own seventies trek across Australia's Red Centre.

Of course, this particular adventurer's twist was that she did it by camel, or, to be accurate, on foot for most of the way: an epic 2700km journey that she would go on to write a book from and which would spin the celebrity spotlight onto her.

More significantly, she would become something of a role-model to other nomads wanting to explore the far reaches of the outer world while potentially also getting in touch with the deep recesses of the inner.

WHEN YOU ARE BORN and raised on a cattle station, the smell of dust and dry heat are an inherent element of day-to-day life that is virtually impossible to escape.

These sensorial memories may become so overwhelming and deeply engrained in one's psyche that they can permeate a person's body and soul, travelling with them through their life, maybe even determining decisions they make.

Robyn Davidson remembers these smells.

Born on 6 September 1950, she spent her childhood years on a small cattle station, 'Stanley Park', in Miles, Queensland.

Three hundred and twenty kilometres west-northwest of Brisbane, this early life was an isolated one for Robyn, her older sister and mother, but they did what they could to keep themselves occupied, her mother determined that the girls grow up as cultured as possible, even given their isolated circumstances, doing whatever was within her power to accomplish this.

This isolation is not for everyone.

It can wear even the strongest souls down, pushing them into dark places where even darker thoughts arise—thoughts that can lead to irreversible actions of drastic consequence.

When Robyn was just eleven years old her mother committed suicide.

Struggling in the aftermath of the death of his wife, Robyn's grieving father was at something of a loss as to how to care for his daughters. Her older sister, already working as a nurse, was not such an issue as she was relatively able to fend for herself, but what would he do about caring for and rearing the younger Robyn without the aid of his wife?

Compounding his misery, the region the station was situated in was suffering a severe drought, making times financially difficult.

His world seemingly crumbling on most fronts, Robyn's father sold the property and they moved to Brisbane. Thinking that she would be better brought up under the watch of a woman, he sent Robyn to live with her aunt Gillian, his twin sister. Although a wonderful woman, being unmarried and with no experience of children, she proved, in Robyn's own words, 'somewhat hopeless' at bringing up a teenage girl, which is not to detract from the kind action of taking her niece into her home!

Robyn attended a girls' boarding school where she did well academically, in particular enjoying music, for which she received a scholarship that was never taken up. Finding zoology of interest, she considered studying it, but her interest waned.

Restless, she hopped a truck: destination, Sydney.

In this exciting urban jungle, Robyn adopted something of a 'feral life', forced to become street-smart as she learned to care for herself in a city relatively huge compared to the isolated life she had spent much of her younger years living and then her more recent time in the much smaller Brisbane.

Stumbling into a job at a gambling club, illegal at the time and run by criminals, she enjoyed the edginess and danger—at least to some degree—of such an illicit life, although eventually this involvement with a criminal element became uncomfortable for her and she wanted to be free of it.

The question, of course, was 'How could she do this?'

Despite not having had much contact with her father since her mother's death, he was the first person she considered reaching out to for help. On some deep level she must have felt a sense of daughterly confidence that, no matter how much time had elapsed between them seeing each other, the bottom line was that she was still his child...and he was still her father...a bond not easily broken.

Robyn wrote to him and he responded with typical paternal care, ready to take action. Driving all the way to Sydney, he collected his daughter and drove her back to the safety of Brisbane.

The nomad in Robyn, however, was now fully awakened, and despite the salvation from a precarious situation her father had offered, she soon felt her inquisitive nature urging her onwards in search of some new adventure.

Unable to resist the call any longer, in 1973 she made plans to leave Brisbane.

As a child she had fantasised about taking a solo expedition, carrying with her just a few possessions, and it seemed that the time had finally come to fulfil this dream. Deciding she wanted to explore the desert, she headed to Alice Springs, thinking this the perfect place to potentially launch such an exploit.

Alice Springs is located almost smack-bang in the centre of the Australian continent, 1200km from the nearest ocean and 1500km from the nearest major city. It has a large indigenous population and even in the 1970s still had a reputation of being something of a frontier town.

Arriving there with six dollars, a single suitcase and her dog, Davidson got a job in a pub, and after a little settling in began formulating a plan involving the possible use of feral camels to conduct her proposed desert trek.

She spent several years working in the Alice, continuing to plan her trip and learning how to ride a camel. The time Robyn spent there was an eye-opening experience in many ways, even after having lived the kind of life she had in Sydney. Given the nature of the town, it was impossible not to encounter at some point the more unsavoury elements and activities, and she was particularly appalled at the way indigenous people were treated.

Still not enough advanced in her trek plans to take action, out of the blue came a man, or two, who would propel Robyn on her journey.

Sallay Mahomet was an Afghan dealer in camels to Arabian countries. Befriending Robyn, Mahomet handed her the keys to allow her to live her dream, offering to provide the camel transportation Robyn so desperately needed if her desert journey was to ever get off the ground.

She also met Rick Smolan, a photographer who had connections to *National Geographic*. Talking with him of her 'dream trek', Rick was excited at the prospect of such, encouraging her to approach the magazine for funding.

Some correspondence, and four thousand dollars later, she was off, bound by the promise to *National Geographic* of writing an article that would describe her journey, to be submitted upon the completion of her trip, with accompanying photos taken at regular intervals by Smolan.

Years later, Robyn would admit she was 'uncomfortable' with the notion of this deal with *National Geographic* as it made her appear to have sold out commercially.

However, it seems likely that had she not negotiated the deal the extended result years later of a more detailed account of her trek might never have taken off without the exposure the original article initially gained her because of its inclusion in *National Geographic*.

Whatever the case, after years of dreaming and planning, her ambitious undertaking finally commenced in 1977.

Accompanied by her dog, Diggity, and four camels (Dookie, Bub, Zeleika and Goliath), Robyn headed into the desert, bound for the far-west coast of the continent. While not necessarily a route of her choice, her agreement with *National Geographic* required some semblance of a beginning, middle and end to the journey, which effectively would become Alice Springs at one end and Hamelin Pool, south of Carnarvon, in WA, at the other.

And a whole lot of desert in between.

Robyn's momentous journey took place over the next eight months. Much of it was on foot, up to 30km a day, a decision driven partially by the fear that if she rode aboard one of the camels too much of the time, she might be thrown and end up in the middle of the outback, injured, with no way of securing aid.

More importantly than acting as steeds, however, these amazing beasts would prove themselves invaluable in acting as water carriers for her journey, something she could clearly not survive without.

Robyn made contact with the Pitjantjatjara tribe during her trip and was thus able to get a more realistic and traditional insight into indigenous life, far removed from the distorted view she had witnessed in Alice Springs. She learned about bush tucker and the dreamtime, and finally was able to experience indigenous peoples living on the land in the way they had for millennia.

Most of the time, however, she was alone.

Rick Smolan met up with her periodically to visually document the experience, but outside of these infrequent meetings, it was an almost entirely solo expedition, just as Robyn had planned.

During these long stretches of solitude, Robyn found herself at the mercy of a plethora of emotional, mental and spiritual states—from euphoric joy one moment to the depths of despair in the next.

And what the solitude did bring was time, and plenty of it, to write...and write...and write.

Taking notes for her article, she recorded as many aspects of the journey as possible, covering both the more obvious physical elements and also the emotional response she had to her trek and the environment through which she travelled. She wrote of the indigenous peoples she met and their lives and ways; of the myriad landscapes she crossed; of the flora and fauna; and of the constant whirl of thoughts that passed through her mind about herself and the world around her.

From the moment she took that first step from a town in the dead, red centre of Australia until months later when she first saw the welcoming deep blue of the Indian Ocean, it was a truly extraordinary journey.

In 1978, her article was published in *National Geographic* and received much attention, its runaway success providing the impetus to write a full account of the journey.

Tracks was the result.

This detailed account of Robyn's trek would go on to be an international bestseller, prize-winning travel memoir (she was the first woman to win the *Thomas Cook Travel Book Award*) and would ultimately go on to be labelled a cult book in terms of travel writing.

The journey she related in Tracks would also set in stone the nomadic life she revelled in, and that would continue for a large chunk of the decades that followed.

Davidson remained in the public eye, on and off, on the back of that first remarkable journey and the writings that followed.

She found herself more prominently thrust into the limelight when involved in a relationship in the mid-eighties with Salman Rushdie during the time he wrote *The Satanic Verses*.

This lasted several years, something it is reported she remembers fondly, despite it being publicised, at least at times, as somewhat tempestuous.

The publishing of *Tracks* would also mark the beginning of decades of more exotic travels for Davidson, most notably in India and Tibet, in what would remain a nomadic existence.

Although she would settle at times in the UK, India and Australia, it would not be until much later in life that she would put down something resembling roots.

Now in her sixties, Robyn lives mostly in Australia where she lectures, occasionally writes for publications such as the highly regarded *The Monthly*, and has done the writer's festivals circuit.

A film is to be made of her landmark book and is scheduled to begin shooting in the Spring of 2012.

Gayle Shan

1976-

In an instant—a flashing, blinding, painful misstep in the greater scheme of things—life can be turned on its head.

Some of the most basic things identified with a 'normal' life go spinning off into the past, and the future is suddenly a great unknown or laden with the burden of fateful happenings.

Yet even such dramatic, life-changing moments like these pass, especially when there exists equal quantities of courage, love and determination within a person, and in those around them, to help lift them from darkness and despair.

In the recent past, one woman in particular would rise to this challenge.

With her indomitable spirit she would not permit anything to get in the way of her love of the outback, or the man she loved,

standing up and taking the challenge of a new life against almost
irrational odds.

THE VALLEY OF LAGOONS lies about 150kms northwest of Townsville, just over halfway between Mackay and Cairns in far northern Queensland, with the Burdekin River neatly bisecting it.

It was in this idyllic-sounding place that Gayle Atkinson was born in 1976.

Her grandfather, Monty, had brought the property back in 1963, and with his son, Alan, developed a successful cattle business for which they were well known and respected by other graziers in the region.

Spending her younger years at the Valley, Gayle left to get her secondary education at boarding school, but the seventeen-year-old came racing home as soon as she had graduated, eager to be back helping out around the station once again.

At the age of twenty-one, Gayle went to Charters Towers to participate in a 'campdrafting' event being held there. 'Campdrafting' is a unique Australian form of rodeo involving a horse-rider and cattle, and requiring an inordinate degree of skill.

During that particular campdrafting event, Gayle met a man a few years her junior who caught her eye, and her heart. His name was Mac Shann and he hailed from a large property, Myall Springs, some six hours south of the Valley.

It was one of those magical comings together where a rapport quickly developed as they revealed their common loves of horses, cattle and the part of the country they lived in.

Not long after, Mac began doing some mustering on Gayle's father's property, giving him the opportunity to spend more time with her, plus offering the chance to get to know the family he hoped one day would become his in-laws.

He quickly proved to be something 'out of the ordinary' from other men Gayle had met on the land. After long days out on the muster, he would surprise both her and her family by coming to the kitchen and helping out with meal preparation, much to the delight and slight envy of her sisters, who wished they could snag such a boyfriend!

The time would come for Gayle and Mac to formalise their love by marrying, and nearly a year after their betrothal, in September 2000, Alan presented the couple with a fantastic opportunity that would allow them to do all they things they loved best.

Having bought a new 12,000ha property just north of Moranbah, 'Cantaur Park', he offered it to his daughter and son-in-law to manage, something they accepted with relish.

It was hard work, something they were both used to, and a lot of responsibility, but the Shanns threw themselves into this new venture, and their ongoing efforts were eventually rewarded with a thriving cattle-breeding business.

In most ways life couldn't have been better, and with the business doing well Gayle and Mac decided to complete some much-needed maintenance about the property.

One particular task requiring attention was fencing.

On one side of the house a fence had been started and never finished and it seemed the perfect time to do something about it.

Deciding to pull it out and replace it with a sturdy steel structure, they enlisted the aid of a friend, Andy Griffin, and got to work. Mac set himself to operate a post-hole digger attached to a tractor, while Gayle took on the task of shovelling soil away from the auger bit as it broke its way through the dirt.

What was to happen next will in all likelihood remain a blur of sheering pain and metallic fury for Gayle for the rest of her life.

As Mac continued to work the digger, his industrious wife somehow mistimed her digging and her glove became caught in the shaft that runs the auger.

Instant catastrophe.

Gayle's body was flung around like a rag doll, underscored by the most horrifying tearing, rending noise. Mac slammed the machine off and bolted to his wife, who lay unconscious, a bloody mangled mess.

In a heartbeat, Mac instantly assessed this as a life and death situation.

He ran to the house to call '000' as Andy carried Gayle inside.

Mac returned to the location of the accident, and, not finding them there, was able to track their journey by the trail of blood leading back inside the property. He raced inside to find his beloved wife, inert, on a single bed covered with a blanket.

Amazingly, yet alarmingly, Gayle regained consciousness at this point and even through the agonising pain was asking why she couldn't move her right arm.

Peering under the blanket revealed the answer.

Where there should have been a healthy limb...was a bloody hole.

Leaving Mac to try and offer Gayle comfort through the ugly miasma of pain and fear that were overwhelming her, Andy went in search of the severed limb, finding it near where they had been working. He removed it from its clothing, and even in the terrible state it was, placed it in the freezer in some vain hope it might be saved and later reattached.

Then began the excruciating two hour wait for the medical services to arrive—an ambulance from Moranbah, helicopter from Rockhampton and the Flying Doctor Service from Townsville.

During the time, the Shann's nearest neighbour, Robyn Newbury, did her best to keep Gayle alive, administering painkillers and relaying as much information as possible via radio to the approaching medical staff. This proved crucial, with them feeding her instructions that would help her preserve the injured woman's life as it seemed to slowly ebb away through the gaping hole in her trunk.

Given the main danger to Gayle was possible death due to loss of blood, without the aid of medical equipment, Robyn used her bare hands to locate the blood vessels that required pinching and hold them together til they clotted.

When the doctors arrived, despite Robyn's gargantuan efforts, the prognosis was grim. Working for two hours they placed Gayle into an induced coma, doing all in their power to seal off arteries and blood vessels to give her the best chance possible of surviving the two-hour flight to Townsville.

Before loading Robyn aboard her mercy flight dash to hospital, they suggested Mac do something that seemed impossible to him—to say goodbye to his wife.

As much as he hoped they could save her, there was enough of a tough realist in Mac to accept the possibility that this could be his last moment with Gayle alive, so he did as suggested, regardless the torture he felt at doing such.

Watching her departure, he then prepared to make the four-hour drive with Alan to Townsville, with the dark cloud hanging over them the whole journey that they might arrive to find she had not made it.

This was not, however, Gayle Shann's time to die.

Surviving the journey, as her vital signs steadied over the next few weeks and she slowly came out of the danger zone, she underwent major surgery.

The difficulty of this lay in the fact that the nerves on the right side were still functional and normal, and yet on the left, where she still had an arm, they were completely destroyed. Her other injuries—broken ribs, a broken nose, a broken leg, multiple lacerations—paled in comparison to the notion of her being armless.

The doctors toiled away for nearly seventeen hours and in a world-first surgical technique managed to harvest nerves from the healthy right side, grafting them to the left.

When Gayle awoke, it was to a new world, at least in terms of mobility. She was alive, thankfully, with her family around her, but without a right arm...and with a left that, despite the surgeon's brave attempts, might remain inert forever.

This was a bitter pill to swallow for them all, but Gayle did all she could to remain on top of this difficult new reality, smiling bravely through such a grim period of her life and glad at least to be alive.

Recovering from such trauma took time, but Gayle was eventually cleared to leave the hospital, and it was straight back to 'Cantaur Park' where finally the enormity of what had happened struck them both.

Had she only lost one arm, Gayle could still have functioned and lived a relatively normal life.

But effectively losing both?

This double whammy presented major difficulties, most especially in the outback given the tough, physical life of running a cattle station. If it wasn't a bitter enough pill to swallow that she could no longer ride her beloved horses, basic things like eating, reading and navigating the house were suddenly tasks almost beyond her.

Of course, as one might expect from a loving man who had already proved himself in years gone by as much more than just a typical supportive partner, Mac was there to help in every way possible. He quickly learned to perform all the basic tasks that she herself could no longer do, such as eating, washing and dressing. He also was required to act as something of a nursemaid because her arm required moving every half hour during her sleep.

For them both, the nights became a challenge, the chance of real, uninterrupted sleep no longer an option, and yet through such trials, the couple soldiered on, with Gayle adapting as much as possible to her changed life.

They altered the way the property worked in every way they could to allow her to return to some semblance of 'normality'. Gates were modified so she could get them open and closed; the local community chipped in with a considerable sum of money to transform the house so she could navigate it more easily and safely; she learned to drive with her feet; and they modified a motorbike so she could help with the mustering.

Then, without warning, came something of a minor miracle.

Twelve months after the accident, Gayle felt a twinge in her left arm.

Yes, actually 'felt'.

For so long she had carried this dead appendage around with her like some burden, with no feeling in it whatsoever, and then, out of nowhere, there was something. It was only minor, granted, but this was still a breakthrough moment for Gayle in believing that one day the limb might become active again.

Even with this slight revelation, the pain remained, and might always, but offsetting the discomfort was the small joy of Gayle gradually regaining some very limited movement in the limb.

With all the hopes and dreams that come with still being a woman in the prime of her life, and with the possibility that at some point in the not-too-distant future medical breakthroughs could one day see her arm having even more functionality, Gayle Shann carries on with the stuff of life, glad to be alive.

An incredibly brave woman made all the stronger by that which did not kill her…

Since the accident, the Shann's have faced the 'normal' outback challenges anyone in their position would.

Droughts and floods.

Years where their herds flourished; others where they diminished.

Moments where the land they cherished challenged them immensely.

And yet after their horrific ordeal in 2002, the lessons they learned about courage in the face of adversity surely hold them in good stead against almost any obstacle or ordeal that might come their way.

Despite having been to the very threshold of death and back, Gayle Shann remains one of our toughest, bravest and more inspiring outback Amazons.

Bibliography

AAP, *Author Sara Henderson dead*, 30 Apr 2005, SMH, 18 Sep 2011 <http://www.smh.com.au/news/Books/Author-Sara-Hendersondead/2005/04/29/1114635754314.html>

De Vries, Susanna, *Great Pioneer Women of the Outback*, 2005, Harper Collins, Australia

Duff, Eamon, *Sara was my mum, so I'm going to her funeral*, 1 May 2005, SMH, 2 Sep 2011 <http://www.smh.com.au/news/People/Sara-was-mymum/2005/04/30/1114635787518.html>

Forrest, Peter, *They of the Never Never, Occasional Papers No 18*, 1990, Northern Territory Library Service, 14 Aug 2011

Garland, Maurie, *The Trials of Isabella Mary Kelly*, 2012, Brolga Publishing, Australia <http://www.ntl.nt.gov.au/__data/assets/pdf_file/0017/25046/occpaper18.pdf>

Hasluck, Alexandra, Molloy, *Georgiana (1805–1843)*, Australian Dictionary of Biography, National Centre of Biography, ANU, 21 Jun 2011 <http://adb.anu.edu.au/biography/molloy-georgiana-2467/text3305>

Isaacs, Jennifer, *Pioneer Women of the Bush and Outback*, 2009, New Holland, Australia

James, Melinda, *A tribute to an outback pioneering legend*, 13 Mar 2006, ABC, 18 Jun 2011 <http://www.abc.net.au/stateline/nt/content/2006/s1606129.htm>

Kovacic, Leonarda, Parker, *Catherine (Katie) Langloh (1856-1940)*, The Australia Women's Register, 18 May 2004, The National Foundation for Australian Women (NFAW), Jul 14 2011 <http://www.womenaustralia.info/biogs/AWE0959b.htm>

Muir, Marcie, Stow, *Catherine Eliza Somerville (Katie) (1856–1940)*, Australian Dictionary of Biography, National Centre of Biography, ANU, 29 Sep 2011 <http://adb.anu.edu.au/biography/stow-catherine-eliza-somerville-katie-8691/text15205>

O'Neill, Sally, *Gunn, Jeannie (1870–1961)*, Australian Dictionary of Biography, National Centre of Biography, ANU, 21 Jun 11 <http://adb.anu.edu.au/biography/gunn-jeannie-6506/text11163>

Pollard, Jane, *Review: No Place for a Woman, The Autobiography of Outback Publican, Mayse Young*, Jessie Street National Women's Library Newsletter, Vol 13, No 2, May 2002, Jessie Street National Women's Library, 18 Sep 2011 <http://www.nationalwomenslibrary.org/forms/newsletter_may02.pdf>

Reece, Bob, *The Irishness of Daisy Bates*, 18 Oct 2009, The Durack Lecture, 03 Oct 2011 <http://www.irishheritage.net/durack2009.pdf>

Ryan, Lyndall, *Review of Marilyn Lake's biography of Faith Bandler, Faith Bandler, Gentle Activist*, Australian Humanities Review, 22 Sep 2011 <http://www.australianhumanitiesreview.org/archive/Issue-May-2003/ryan.html>

Stephens, Tony, *Escapee from Nazi fought for Aborigines*, 14 Sep 2009, SMH, 20 Sep 2011 <http://www.smh.com.au/national/obituaries/escapee-from-nazis-fought-for-aborigines-20090913-fmad.html>

Sturkey, Douglas, *Withnell, Emma Mary (1842–1928)*, Australian Dictionary of Biography, National Centre of Biography, ANU, 21 Jun 11 <http://adb.anu.edu.au/biography/withnell-emma-mary-4880/text8163>

Wikipedia contributors, *Georgiana Molloy*, Wikipedia, The Free Encyclopedia, 10 Sep 2011, Wikipedia, The Free Encyclopedia, 13 Jun 2011 <http://en.wikipedia.org/wiki/Georgiana_Molloy>

Wilkinson, Jane, *Gunn, Jeannie (Mrs Aeneas) (1870-1961)*, Australian Women's Register, 23 Sep 2003, The National Foundation for Australian Women (NFAW), Jul 14 2011 <http://www.womenaustralia.info/biogs/AWE0562b.htm>

Williams, Sue, *Women of the Outback*, 2009, Penguin Books, Australia

Unknown, *Makers of Western Australia: (15) Emma Mary Withnell*, Western Mail (Perth, WA: 1885 - 1954) 13 Aug 1925: 1 Supplement: Regular supplement - Pictorial Section, 20 Sep 2011

Unknown, *Current Literature*, the Sydney Morning Herald (NSW: 1842 - 1954), 1 Dec 1934: 12, 17 Sep 2011

Unknown, *Georgiana's Story*, The Argus (Melbourne, Vic: 1848 - 1956) 8 Sep 1934: 4, 17 Sep 2011

Unknown, *Mayse Young Farewelled in Darwin*, 30 Mar 2006, ABC News, 25 Jun 2011 <http://www.abc.net.au/news/2006-03-30/mayse-young-farewelled-in-darwin/1720670>

Unknown, *Georgiana Molloy*, date unknown, Australia's South West, 30 Jun 2011 <http://www.australiassouthwest.com/en/Destination/History/Explorers_and_Settlement/Pages/Georgiana_Molloy.aspx>

Unknown, *Faith Bandler*, World Peoples Blog, 21 Sep 2011 <http://word.world-citizenship.org/wp-archive/467>

Unknown, *Daisy Bates*, Flinders Ranges Research, 25 Jun 2011 <http://www.southaustralianhistory.com.au/bates.htm>

Unknown, *Faith Bandler*, Australians, ABC, 20 June 2011 <http://www.abc.net.au/schoolstv/australians/f.bandler.htm>

Unknown, *Faith Bandler*, Oxfam Australia, 12 Jun 2011 <http://www.oxfam.org.au/act/diy-campaigning/can-one-person-change-the-world/faith-bandler>

Unknown, *Life and Times of an Australian Collector- Catherine Langloh Parker, Selected Tales from Oral Traditions*, 8 Jun 2011 <http://enargea.org/tales/Australian/Katie_Langloh_Parker.html>

Unknown, *Emma Mary Whitnell,* Pandora Australia's web archive, 14 Jun 2011 <http://pandora.nla.gov.au/pan/95993/20090319-1853/now-andthen.noadsfree.com/withnell.html>

OUTBACK WOMEN

Paul Bugeja

ISBN 9781925367744	Qty	
RRP	AU$24.99	.....
Postage within Australia	AU$5.00	.....
	TOTAL★ $_____	
	★ All prices include GST	

Name:...

Address: ....

....

Phone:...

Email: ....

Payment: ❏ Money Order ❏ Cheque ❏ Amex ❏ MasterCard ❏ Visa

Cardholders Name:..

Credit Card Number: ....

Signature:..

Expiry Date: ....

Allow 7 days for delivery.

Payment to: Marzocco Consultancy (ABN 14 067 257 390)
                  PO Box 12544
                  A'Beckett Street, Melbourne, 8006
                  Victoria, Australia
                  admin@brolgapublishing.com.au

BE PUBLISHED

Publish through a successful publisher.
Brolga Publishing is represented through:
• **National** book trade distribution, including sales,
marketing & distribution through **Macmillan Australia.**
• **International** book trade distribution to
   • The United Kingdom
   • North America
   • Sales representation in South East Asia
• **Worldwide e-Book distribution**

For details and inquiries, contact:
Brolga Publishing Pty Ltd
PO Box 12544
A'Beckett St VIC 8006

Phone: 0414 608 494
markzocchi@brolgapublishing.com.au
ABN: 46 063 962 443
(Email for a catalogue request)